ANTI DOTE TO ANTI DOPE

A Woman's Journey to the Light at the End of the Tunnel

NARCY ELMOGHAZY

TABLE OF CONTENTS

Introduction 1

Chapter 1: My family 3

Chapter 2: Old Fashion 10

Chapter 3: Egypt 15

Chapter 4: Cancer 22

Chapter 5: Behind Closed Doors 26

Chapter 6: Princess 30

Chapter 7: Run Away 33

Chapter 8: Short Shorts 36

Chapter 9: Train Choo Choo 38

Chapter 10: Suicide Attempt 45

Chapter 11: Kitty 47

Chapter 12: Georgia 50

Chapter 13: His Boys 54

Chapter 14: Prostitution 57

Chapter 15: Snitch 61

Chapter 16: Disowned 63

Chapter 17: Abortion 65

Chapter 18: Jump Out Boys 68

Chapter 19: Diamante 72

Chapter 20: Inside job 74

Chapter 21: R.A.D.S(Reactive attachment disorder) 78

Chapter 22: Living but not Really Living 82

Chapter 23: Weirdo 86

Chapter 24: DEJAVU 91

Chapter 25: Notasulga AL. Police 93

Chapter 26: Emergency Court Hearing 98

Chapter 27: Bate 101

Chapter 28: Breaking point 109

Chapter 29: Life or Death 116

Chapter 30: Atlanta Ga. Temptation 119

Chapter 31: Transformation 127

Chapter 32: Sumo Cocaine Addict 132

Chapter 33: Chevy Tahoe 136

Chapter 34: Gay pride in Austin Texas 138

Chapter 35: My Drink, Got got 140

Chapter 36: Cat and Mouse 143

Chapter 37: Twenty-nine and Dying 146

Chapter 38: Officially a Uhaul Employee 148

Chapter 39: We Met an Angel 151

Chapter 40: Recap 157

Chapter 41: Not by coincidence 159

Chapter 42: Pizza and Taz 164

Chapter 43: C. Williams 167

Chapter 44: Another Devilish Experience 171

Chapter 45: A Woman and her Dog 173

Chapter 46: Process of Elimination 176

Chapter 47: Own the Streets or the Streets will Own You 182

Chapter 48: Bullies 188

Chapter 49: Intuitive 192

Chapter 50: Red Shirts Angels 195

Chapter 51: Busy people 198

Chapter 52: Process 201

Chapter 53: Sentimental stranger 203

Chapter 54: B.O.B. 206

Chapter 55: Finally at Peace 210

INTRODUCTION

I have a purpose; we all do. It took me 37 years to finally realize my purpose on this earth. In this book, I share with you the trials and tribulations I have been through. The goal is to help you learn from my mistakes, make the right decisions, and avoid repeating the same mistakes that I have made in the past. Life is short, and tomorrow is not promised. Some of the things you are about to read may appear hard to believe. It takes my present journey to understand. I'm a living testimony; I have the conviction that things can get better. I'm desperate to share my story with you guys. The things that have occurred in my life were all a part of the Divine plan. My life's journey will inspire everyone, irrespective of race, color or status. It's my hope it helps heal the broken, and spread the love that is needed for humanity as a whole to become better.

This book is for the black sheep, outcasts, drug addicts, alcoholics, molested, prostitutes, and kids growing up in foster care, homeless, non-believers, hypocrites, but most of all the people who are and always will be defined by their past. I've been there. I've done it. I don't feel any shame about it, and I'm not judgmental. Most importantly, this book is written for my two children. I may not be able to tell you the truth, but at least you will be able to read it. I love you two dearly, and I truly apologize from the depths of my heart for not being the mother you two needed. Just know that I love you. Until we meet again. Gods blessed us with an amazing world. Sadly, however, a lot of us are taking it for granted. We need to remember where we come from, because when it's over, it's really just begun. I want to make it through these gates. You deserve to make it through those gates too.

Chapter 1

MY FAMILY

My name is Narghsanne Elmogahzy, but everyone calls me Narcy. Growing up, I couldn't pronounce my real name, so I made up "Narcy." My father bought me a plant when I was a child and told me that I was named after it. It was an Egyptian white flower, to me it held an awful odor. Truly, I wasn't happy about it, but now that I'm older, I have learned to love it. One of my biggest faults in life was the urge to please people. As long as everyone around me was happy, I thought I was. I was born on October 7, 1985, in Raleigh, North Carolina, at Duke Hospital, in Durham County. My father was (May his soul rest in the bosom of the Lord) from Mansoura Egypt. My father grew up poor, helping his mother, his brothers and his sisters. His father died early in his life. He had three brothers, and three sisters. He was a twin but his twin sister died at birth. My father had always been the funniest person that ever existed in my eyes. Whenever he entered a room, he automatically lit the entire room up. He was a God to me; he was my hero.

My father came to the United States when he was 23 years old. Before his departure, his mother had packed his suit cases. He was definitely a mama's boy. My father had a favorite soup called *Mulukhiyah*. It is the national dish of Egypt. It's made by cooking a large amount of finely chopped jute, which is a green leaf vegetable with a distinctively bitter flavor. My father's mother was determined to make sure her son had plenty of it, so she cooked it, and packed ten bags of it in sealed freezer bags and packed it in his suitcase. When my father arrived at the airport in the United States, he was quickly detained in a waiting room until the guards searched his entire luggage. Four hours later, they found out it wasn't Marijuana but a soup from Egypt. At this time, my father couldn't speak English, so this poor guy was panicking—a sight I would have loved to see. I laugh every time I think about it. My father studied and devoted his life to his work and his family the best way he could. The first job my father got in the USA was as a bartender. I learned about this many years later. Growing up, my father was anti-alcohol, so finding this out was a surprise to me.

My father met my mother in North Carolina, while he was studying. From what I can remember she was a free spirit, American white woman, who came from a broken home. My father wanted better for her, so he encouraged her to get her GED. He helped tutor her. My mother and my father ended up getting married, and they gave birth to Lil Elmo, my elder brother. I was born shortly after. We are only a year apart. Right after I was born, my father decided to relocate us to Auburn AL.

My father ended up completing school, and became a professor of Textiles at Auburn University. It's one of the most profound colleges in the USA, and well-known for college football. My father was always at work, studying, and traveling on business trips. If I recall, my brother and I spent a lot of time with my mother up until we were three and four years old. My mother had a lot of friends and we were always around them while my father was working to provide for us. There's not much I can remember during the few years we lived with my mother.

My first encounter as a child being molested was by a white older male from my mother's side of the family. All I can remember was sitting on a riding lawn mower, riding around the yard for hours as this man abused me. My father was probably oblivious about this incident. He was always consumed with his work. I have questions I know I will never get true answers. Growing up, I was told my mother was on drugs and alcohol. I didn't know I would find the truth out 37 years later.

My parents ended up losing custody of us. Things were unstable, my brother ended up drinking out of a coke can which had cigarette buds and ashes. This made him sick, and the department of children services got involved. My father fought with the state and regained custody of both my brother and me. During this fight to regain custody, we were placed in foster care. My second encounter with child molestation occurred in foster care. My mother didn't have a chance against a professor at Auburn University. When she realized she wasn't getting us back, she went into shock, and was admitted in a hospital. Then my father alienated her from us, and kept us away from her. I knew he thought it was the right thing to do at this point in my life. I had no clue what was going on. I was just a baby. My father was still consumed by his studies and work, so my brother and I barely got to see him.

I got to have a conversation with my biological mother twenty three years later, and she told me she was never on drugs or alcohol, and that my father got abusive, married her for the green card, and wouldn't let her see us. My mom said every holiday she drove by our house with hopes that we would be looking out the window and see her. She said that she would dress me up in cabbage patch doll clothes, and swaddle me as a baby. Then she would lay me down in one of the dresser drawers right next to her bed, stating that if I made as little as a peep, she would be right there by my side to make sure I was fine. I know both of my parents loved us. They were just two opposites with different opinions and perspectives about things.

During this time, my father was best friends, with this Egyptian family. We would call the mother (auntie), the father (uncle), their daughter (big sis), and their son (big bro). Auntie became somewhat of a mother figure for us. This family was the only family around when my father and my mother were still married. The true definition of family was the love and sense of belonging they shared with my brother and me. Aunt became my father's go to when it came to babysitting us while he worked and studied, which was all the time. My father made sure to buy me the biggest jar of peanut butter from the store every morning before he dropped us off at aunties' house. Peanut butter was my absolute favorite food ever. As long as I had peanut butter, I was set. During this time, both my brother and I probably were four and five. This family remained our family since we were born. However, because of unfortunate circumstances which you will learn later on, we lost contact. This would be the last time I honestly felt genuinely loved and safe as a child. I miss this family to this day with all my heart.

I was a cute little talkative, and when I say talkative, I mean I would talk anyone's head off about things a child my age shouldn't know or talk about. I remember getting in trouble a lot. I had this nickname, *nosey nara*, because I entered adults' conversations I had no business entering, but I wasn't taught differently. I didn't understand boundaries. I know my brother and I blocked out a ton, because the shit we lived through being so innocent and young—no kid should ever have to experience it. My brother and I had fun with each other sexually all the time. We had seen something growing up, and weren't told it was inappropriate for children our age to practice. We thought it was normal, and it continued until we were 15 and 16. I had long, straight, dark brown hair that grew to my knees, with the prettiest hazel eyes that people still compliment to this day. I remember auntie having to cut my hair off one afternoon because I had lice. One thing she used to always do was play with my hair, and it felt so good. I felt relaxed about the experience, and sometimes I would fall asleep. Auntie was upset when she had to chop it all off.

My brother and I could have been taken care of better. Whenever auntie got us, we were dirty, and she would have to save the day and clean us up. They truly adored my brother and me. We also adored them. This family was the only ones I knew I could get real answers to questions I had about my biological mother growing up. I think everyone just tried to protect my brother and me, but sometimes it just really felt like they were trying to protect my father's name. I would always go to the lake with my dad, my brother, and this family.

Narrator Insert:

It makes a difference when you're sober about the things you can recall about your childhood. God has led me on this journey, and I'm eternally grateful. Being homeless on these streets in Austin Texas has opened my eyes to the true meaning of living. What's the essence of living when you're not really living? I remain grateful to God I'm finally living. I get tired and unable to rest, but the positive outweighs the negatives. It brings tears to my eyes when I remember that after all of the drug use and alcohol abuse I put myself through for 13 years, I'm finally free. Now I have peace and contentment in my heart. It leaves my soul content regardless of the pain in my past. I need you, my reader, to learn from this.

My father and *unc* would always throw so much food on the grill, and everyone around us as well as strangers would eat. My father loved everyone, irrespective of their color, gender, religion, or beliefs. I know I inherited that trait. We always had a watermelon cut wide open for everyone to eat on our picnic table, and it became a fixture in all of our lake ventures. Everyone would be speaking Arabic, and at this point in my childhood, I could understand the Arabic language, but I could not articulate the language well, because as a child, I already had an Alabama accent which interfered with the Arabic. Arabic will always and forever be a beautiful language to me. The older I got the more I became the Arab redneck, and of course I was also, *tickle me elmo*. People would tickle me till I pissed on myself. It's unfortunate that the experiences I've lived through growing up would tarnish the way I felt for most of my pre-teen and teen years. Honestly, after 37 years later, I have realized in every culture, every background, and race, there are good and there are bad situations. This book doesn't discriminate on any specific race because with age I have learned love is what this world needs to make the difference to help our humanity. I thrive to be part of the solution not the problem.

My father did silly things like squeezing my nose and giving my booger to my brother. He would act like he was picking his nose and he would reach behind my ear and pull out this big ball of gum. At the time, I really thought it was a booger, but that was just my father being a goober. My father had no filter.

I'm learning with age that I'm not so different after all. One of the things I miss that my father would do was cuff my arm in his, and we would walk together. He called it *anga gee*. I do it now with my future husband. I'll tell you all about him soon. It's cute because my soon to be husband will walk up to me and ask me if I want to *anga gee*, and it warms the hell out of my heart

Chapter 2

OLD FASHION

▬▬▬

My father was old fashion, and had the view that a woman should take care of the home, and the family. My father and Unc organized a wedding party in New Orleans for my father and his new wife. We called her Nanny. She was an Egyptian American and had a history degree. She was beautiful. She came as a packaged deal. She already had a son by another man. We called her son Lil Bagdadi—a step grandma we called Sitty. Nanny was beautiful. She had long black hair, and dark big brown eyes. She was extremely intelligent. When it was good in our family, it was really good, but when things went bad, they went to hell.

Narrator insert:

I pray for forgiveness for everyone in my life that caused me pain because I have forgiven everyone. Life is too short, and what truly matters is what happens to us when we leave this world, and God can only be the judge of that.

In the beginning of Nanny and my father's relationship, it was great. Everyone was healthy and looked amazing. My father still worked a lot and we spent a lot of time in New Orleans at Sitty's house. Sitty and Nanny were trying to clean my brother and meup, discipline us, because we weren't disciplined and our father didn't have time to properly care for us, because he was always working. We lost our mother and didn't really understand all the sudden changes that occurred around us. I could only imagine how Lil Baghdadi felt growing up without his father. His story was like ours. Nanny's first husband was an Egyptian who married her, to gain citizenship in the USA. Many years later, I found out Lil Baghdadi's father was already married and had a whole separate family back in his hometown, Egypt. Lil Baghdadi's father's scheme was to become a citizen of the US, then kidnap Lil Baghdadi. He had tried getting on a plane with Lil Baghdadi when he was just a baby, but something happened and he couldn't get on the plane. Nanny caught him, just in time, and got her son back. The bond between Lil Baghdadi and his mother was beautiful and unbreakable—a love and relationship I wish I had with my mother. When Lil Baghdadi came of age, he finally went to Egypt , and met his father and the rest of his family, and they all made amends, right before Lil Baghdadi died a few years later. God rest his beautiful soul. We will talk about this tragedy later on.

My father, Sitty, and Nanny got along in the beginning really well. Sitty would cook Egyptian food every night that reminded my father about life back home with his family in

Egypt. I knew my father missed his family in Egypt, and at last our family started making my father feel at home. We united as a family. The older I become, the more I realize Lil Elmo and I weren't the easiest for the new family to mold (we had been through a lot) into well behaved and well-mannered kids. Growing up as a Muslim, and living accordingly to the norms of the society was something that would take lots of time We were already Muslims though we were not practicing. My father was always at work and didn't have time to teach us. Lil Baghdadi came first when it came to Sitty. Sitty was a die hard Muslim. While we were in New Orleans (the first couple of years of my father and Nanny's marriage), she shoved Islam down our throats. My brother, Lil Baghdadi and I attended Muslim Sunday school, and began learning to recite verses from the Quran. It got to the point that if we didn't have certain verses memorized, We weren't allowed to go anywhere with Nanny, we loved going places with her and Lil Baghdadi. At this time we made a lot of good friends that had kids our age to play with. Moreover, Nanny loved to shop, and she would buy me pretty outfits, and do my hair in pigtails all the time. I absolutely loved it when she French braided my hair.

Nanny loved shopping, and sometimes she would buy things not because we needed them but because they were on sale. She got some really good deals sometimes. She loved buying things for all of our family members in Egypt, and all of my cousins loved it. Nanny had one of the biggest hearts anyone could ever have. She just spent a lot of money and I learned later on that it affected our financial security that my father worked so hard to maintain. Lil Elmo and I really liked getting the happy meals with the toys in it, it most certainly beat the dinner we knew Sitty had prepared for all of us upon our return home, her dinner didn't have a toy.

My father and my step mother ended up having two daughters together. My father absolutely adored them. They were always dressed in Mickey and Minnie Mouse, and usually always matched each other. One sister, whom we called Tomboy—because growing up she was the tougher of the two—didn't care about all the pretty little bows, and flowers all over the ruffled dresses, and the cute little glitter jelly shoes, She cared more about making all of her brothers and sisters happy, and she would give up all her toys if it meant her sister wouldn't cry. We called her sister, Girlie girl, because that's exactly what she was. The two of them were inseparable. Girlie girl was definitely a daddy and nanny's girl while tomboy boy was definitely a Sitty's girl. Sitty absolutely loved Tommy Boy. Girlie Girl was picky and hated getting dirty. I'm not being ugly but she was a prissy little thing. She and I never bonded, not like Tommy boy and I. For the most part all of us got along. Things went south when Lil Elmo and I were caught playing with each other in the toy room at Sitty's house. She started giving us a stern look, and we really thought what we were doing was normal. You can imagine how we feel now that we finally knew that what we were doing was bad. Sitty put Lil Elmo on the bottom bunk, and I was on the top bunk. Lil Baghdadi, Sitty, Tommy Boy, and Girlie Girl slept in this big king-size bed in the center of the bedroom. Right then it was like Lil Elmo and I were different from the rest. It really wasn't a new feeling to us;, our entire lives thus far felt this way. I understood Arabic. I heard Sitty telling family friends about the incident, and those family friends with the kids that Lil Elmo and I just became friends with started avoiding us. We didn't hang out with them as much, their parents were afraid for their kids. My dad wasn't told about any of this. I don't know why. Sitty started treating us like wild dogs when my father wasn't around.

Narrator insert:

Before we go down a road that I dread with my entirety, let me make clear, that everyone in my life at some point is or was a victim of unfortunate circumstances. I still love them all.

Chapter 3

EGYPT

—————

We traveled to Egypt a couple times as a family. It was one of the times Nanny got to be Nanny, and Sitty wasn't around to antagonize the situation. Sitty had a control over her daughter, and that was very unsettling. Whenever Sitty was around, Nanny did as she said. That was another reason Lil Elmo and I always wanted to go wherever Nanny and Lil Baghdadi went. Nanny was a good mother to us when Sitty wasn't around.

We all boarded the Lufthansa airplane and headed to Egypt. Everyone was excited, and my dad was already in Egypt waiting with the rest of our aunts, uncles, and cousins for our arrival. Nanny made sure we took turns sitting at the window to look over the clouds. As we landed in Egypt I watched as our plane glided over the beautiful Nile river on the landing strip—a sight that to me meant freedom because back home with Sitty things really started getting weird.

As we walked out of the terminal, we were greeted by my uncle, Adel. He was my absolute favorite. At this time he was getting sick, and the doctors in Egypt couldn't do the necessary procedures to cure him. Nonetheless, he still had the most loving and upbeat personality of them all. He absolutely loved me and Lil Elmo, and my father and and him were very close. When my uncle Adel finally passed on, my father was in complete shambles. I know my father wished he could have done more for my uncle as far as the medical treatment. My father felt guilty, and wished he would have done more. Then there was my Aunt A and uncle M, and their two kids Boos Boos, and Moe. My Aunt A's husband married a great man that gave them a great lifestyle. However, my aunt, Med, and her husband, Unc Hass, who had three kids, Mada, Summer, and Sarah didn't have a great lifestyle. You could tell the difference between the two families. At times Aunt A acted like she was too good, and wouldn't get dirty. Boos Boos was the same way, and Moe was a momma's boy. His momma made sure he was taken care of. This family was used to being catered for. I remember Boos Boos getting yelled at by my Aunt A all the time; it was funny. I chose to spend the night with Aunt A and Boos Boos every time we visited Egypt because Boos Boos was allowed to do more than my other Aunt allowed her kids to do, and all I wanted was freedom.

Then there was my Aunt Med, and Uncle Hass, who were not as well off, as Aunt A and her family. Nonetheless, Aunt Med was real. She worked hard to keep her family a float and when we were in Egypt, she cooked some of the most amazing meals for us. She was like the momma of our entire family, whenever we visited Egypt, she raised her kids well. All of my cousins helped in the kitchen when it was time to cook, and we all ate together. When it came to cleaning the dishes, we all pitched in and helped. You could tell my Aunt Med was tired. She overdid it sometimes, but that in itself brought her three children up to be extremely smart, and strong.

Sarah, Summer and Ham were her three amazing children. Sarah and Summer were absolutely beautiful, and Ham grew to be one of the strongest, most handsome young men I know. You could tell the difference between both families. You could feel the tension at times, but I was young and didn't understand why. I always thought we all were equal. Then there was my aunt Nag and her husband. We never really got to know her husband. He was always at work, and they lived in Dubai, a completely different city. They were never at the airport waiting for us. They always came later on in our visit. They had a son named Ah. We didn't get to spend as much time as we wanted to with them. Finally, there was Uncle E, Aunt Nad, and Dalula. Aunt Nad was absolutely stunning to me. She was a Russian and tall. Her health condition wasn't too great. Her Arabic wasn't precise; it was broken like mine and my brothers because Russian was her first language.

Nanny was a huge history fanatic. She studied history in school. So she made sure our trip was filled with museums, pyramids, tours of the sphinx, and historic sites. We got to see beautiful mosques. We had to take off our shoes and cover our heads before entering. We were showing respect to God. Living in Egypt for three months was hard for all of us. Our digestive systems had to adjust to the food, and our bodies weren't used to the heat. We all had diarrhea, and couldn't hold any food down. Tommy Boy had it the worst. She would have nose bleeds every time she got too hot. Girlie Girl was just so damn picky. Nanny had her hands full. As I said my, father believed that the woman should take care of the kids, and that's what Nanny did.

Just imagine the stress of getting three kids ready before going anywhere. Moreover, she would have to get her husband's clothes ready every day. Nanny did her best. Nanny did just as much work to keep the home together as best as she could.

We all got lice and I remember Nanny treating everyone's head, and combing the little bugs out of our hair. It took our family a month to adjust to everything in Egypt. My father owned a chalet in Egypt, and it was absolutely beautiful.

Narrator Insert:

My father's chalet had our family name engraved in it, and without my knowledge my brothers and my sisters sold it when my father passed away. When I found out, I questioned my family on Facebook. Not only did Lil Elmo cut me off from the inheritance that my father had left me, he also sold the chalet my father worked extremely hard to leave for me. My siblings knew I wouldn't dare sell what my father worked so hard to leave us as part of the "Elmogahzy" legacy.

This chalet was supposed to be my home when I got older, and my father would tell me this as a child. He would say, "Narcy, you can have whatever you want; you just have to listen." He also told me that no matter what was going on in my life, I would always have a home in Egypt.

Let's talk about the weddings I got to attend in Egypt, I was fortunate to experience some of the most beautiful parties ever. Nanny would take us to all the bridal shops in the states to try on beautiful dresses to prepare us for the weddings we were attending. She made sure all of us looked stunning. Nanny was always selfless, and always wanted my father to be happy. So she did everything in her power to cover every loose end in everything. The weddings were not the traditional wedding you would attend in the states. They lasted two to three days. The woman would attend the henna, which was just for the woman. They would all get together and henna each other. Henna was used to color our hair; it left a burgundy tent, and the red dye would dye the tips of our nails, and we would draw flowers and beautiful designs all over our arms and hands. The men would have their own party. Then there would be the sacrifice of the goat or lamb. At the poorer weddings we attended, they butchered the goat or lamb in their kitchens and there would be blood everywhere. However, there would be a drain in the middle of the kitchen floor that would absorb the blood, and we would boil the head of the goat or lamb and make a broth for the rest of our feast. My absolute favorite would be stuffed grape leaves. It was a blend of rice, ground beef, goat or lamb, and different seasonings. I think I really just enjoyed sitting in Aunt Med's kitchen/dining room while making it together—all of us pitched in.

Then there would be the wedding. The dresses the brides wore were more beautiful and exotic than the brides, that were showed in this t.v. show i use to watch, called, "Gypsy Weddings". Right before the wedding, all the women would go together to a salon, and we would get some of the best treatment. This was the first time I had my eyebrows threaded. Though it hurt, it was the most beautiful eyebrow job I had ever seen. They used old fashioned curlers to braid our hair, which sat on top of a fire to be heated and then curled our hair. In my 37 years of existence, no salon has ever beat the stylists work 'I've been fortunate to experience in Egypt. I dream of getting married in Egypt one of these days.

I smoked my first joint with my cousin Moe in Mansoura, Egypt, on the first floor of his family's chalet in his aunt's apartment while they were out of town. I really just wanted a cigarette, and my cousin told me to come with him. I hit it like

I would a cigarette, but only to realize instantly it wasn't a cigarette. At that moment, I realized I needed to improve my Arabic. All we could hear was Aunt A's screaming from the third floor, "Moe ya wala (which means hey boy) Moe." Moe and I were trying hard to get rid of the hashish smell, and then we hid for about ten minutes, then made it back upstairs. Moe got yelled at. I'm sure my Aunt A was smart enough to put two and two together, she knew what we had just done, but I think she was more worried about my father finding out. So we hung out with her for a few hours.

Boos Boos and I loved talking about boys. Our parents let us go to the "Nadi", (it was the hangout park all the kids and teens would go to, hang out, play tennis, eat ice cream, flirt. Our parents didn't know anything about that). At this time, I was the American white girl that all the boys wanted to get to know and wanted to marry because they wanted to go to America. All the boys tried talking to me. The dream of most people is to live in the USA. I was known as the Mona Lisa. All the guys called me that. Mona Lisa was ugly, back then I didn't know the real beauty Mona Lisa possessed. I was a celebrity in Egypt. I loved the attention. When Boos Boos and I got home from the Nadi, we would wait till her parents fell asleep and then we would sneak into her father's office and sit underneath her father's desk and use the office phone to call boys. We would be so quiet. Moe had our backs. He would look out, and make sure no one was coming. I remember when the style for girls was skirts that were attached to pants. At the time I thought they were stupid, but eight years later in the States they were popular. A lot of things came out in Egypt before the states. I remember listening to Ace of Base, N Sync, Backstreet boys, and Spice girls for the first time in Egypt, and when we returned to the States, the music didn't come out for another year. Egypt had McDonald's, and pizza hut. Everything we had in the states we had in Egypt, and everything in Egypt was of better quality, and affordable. We would visit Egypt every other summer for three months and then return to the States. We all cried when we had to leave, it was bittersweet.

Chapter 4

CANCER

▬▬▬

My father ended up finding a house in Auburn AL, on McKinley Street so we all moved from New Orleans and became a part of the Auburn AL. community. Sitty came with us, but she still owned her house in New Orleans. She was just lonely and she wanted to help Nanny with all the kids. Nanny and my father found out they were pregnant with a little boy. At this time Sitty's true colors started to surface, and Lil Elmo and I learned quickly that playing with each other wasn't normal.

"Kids come downstairs, we have something to talk to you about," my father shouted from downstairs. All of us came running down the stairs and into my father's office. Nanny looked like she had just seen a ghost. My father kept rubbing his eyes and Sitty was trying to get all of us to sit down and be quiet. Then Nanny says, "Kids, I have cancer." Then she got her doctor on the phone and put the conversation on loud speaker. The doctor goes on to say, "Kids, you guys have to help your momma out and be on your best behavior because she is really sick." All of us began crying. My father told us that we would be going back to New Orleans with Nanny and Sitty because Nanny's chemotherapy would be in New Orleans. Nanny and her family knew a few good doctors; they were Muslim Egyptians, really great people. Nanny didn't just have breast cancer; she had lupus, multiple sclerosis, and was in awful health. God bless her soul. Sitty took on the mother role, and honestly i think Sitty was sick too. But she had to be tough. Some years later, they found her dead in her home. I'm not sure how she died but i think Sitty was sick but she was the type of person that she believed if God wanted her, he would take her when it was her time to go. So she continued living her life.

Narrator insert:

I believe in deaths by 3's. When Nanny died, Sitty died, then Lil Baghdadi died too. In order to heal, you must forgive. Your soul deserves, and desires the freedom from those chains that truly hinder your growth. I need to press this. I want everyone to know that no one is bad. We just make bad decisions. Some of us are more fortunate than others, and learn, like Weirdo (my future husband's), and myself. I'm fortunate to have been divinely guided into the right direction and fortunate enough to be given the opportunity to write my wrongs, face my karma, and break generational curses.

Sitty was the type of woman whom while she was married to Nanny's father she wore the sexy sun dresses. She was in fact beautiful, she use to wear her makeup, and do her hair.

Nonetheless, her husband (Nanny's father) had an affair and left her to an American white woman. All Sitty ever tried to do was make Nanny's father happy, but she also was sick mentally and made his life hell. It was like a slap in the face. To her, I'm sure. You will learn later how dysfunctional my family really was, how ungrateful and sorry Nanny's father really was. Nanny's father tried turning Nanny and Nanny's brother against Sitty. Nanny's brother disconnected from them for a while, and then eventually came back around. That's another story in itself. Sitty was hard to get along with, and I now understand why everyone stopped associating with her. I love her but I know she had some mental illness.

My father had to work and all of my stepmom's doctor's appointments were in New Orleans, so we lived at Sitty's while my father stayed in Auburn AL. I hated him for allowing that. Lil Baghdadi got to go with his mom everywhere, and Lil Elmo and I were stuck at the house with Sitty. I mean she really and truly ruined our childhood.

Lil Baghdadi ate better than us. I remember Lil Elmo sneaking a snack cake out of the pantry and Sitty found out it was gone at 2 a.m. (we were probably 10 and 11 years old, and had school the next day). Sitty got both of us out of bed and made us sit at the kitchen table with a plate full of literally a foot high of nutty buddy bars, star crunch cakes, ding dongs, brownies, and peanut butter and jelly sandwiches. We were forced to eat every single crumb off of our plates, or there would be no sleep. If either of us threw up, she filled the plate up again and we were forced to eat the entire plate. Sitty literally made Lil Elmo eat some of his throw up, while she criticized Lil elmo. Lil Baghdadi would always try to take the blame to help us out, but that didn't matter. Sitty didn't care if it was a school night or not; she believed Lil Baghdadi to be perfect, and us to literally be Satan's spawn. There were times she had us wash all the dishes used to make our food, and if a single dish didn't squeak, she returned every single dish we had already cleaned back to the sink, plus the dishes in the dishwasher that were already clean. Sitty was strange. I believed she went too far when it came to some Islamic beliefs because she would make us sleep on our right sides, and if she caught us sleeping on our left sides, we would be woken up by a smack in the face. She believed that sleeping on your right side was like sleeping with the angels, and sleeping on your left side was like sleeping with the devil. She was pretty twisted. She would call us the devil whenever we were caught sleeping on our left sides. We had many sleepless nights. We ended up moving back to Auburn because Nanny was in remission. Auntie and Unc's family came to visit, but that was short-lived because her son, who was like a brother to me, Big bro, stood up for us, and got into it with Nanny and Sitty. Big Bro got really upset with the way Nanny and Sitty mistreated us, and became pissed at them. Finally, someone stood up for us for the first time. The people that tried protecting us were alienated from our lives. We learned quickly no one ever stuck around. I think that was when my father woke up and started paying more attention to what was really going on. It took my father long enough to finally realize he was tired of us being abused. Sadly, that was the day I lost my true family, and any chance of living a normal life. At that point, I knew Lil Elmo and I were fucked, because who were we to confide in and tell what was going on. When we felt unsafe, we had no one. My father was always at work. That is the very first time I questioned God's existence.

Chapter 5

BEHIND CLOSED DOORS

———————

Sitty laid out a dress for me. It was one of her old ones from back in the fifties. I thought it was one of the most hideous dresses ever. We argued about it, and screamed. I couldn't go to school looking like a clown. At this time, the way you dressed and looked determined whether or not you were cool. I wanted to be accepted; that's all I ever wanted. Hell, I already wasn't accepted at home, or by Nanny's family. I just wanted to be normal at school, maybe be a cool kid. Sitty wasn't having it. Sitty went to grab me and tossed me back and forth across the living room floor, until she finally threw me far enough to hit the kitchen table and gashed my head. There was blood everywhere. Our kitchen was right across from the living room, where the kitchen table sat, and it was made out of solid wood.

This didn't stop Sitty from sending me to school. Nanny had started getting sick again and was always in the back room sleeping. Sitty had to force her to drink ensures and slim fasts because her body didn't allow her to hold anything down, so for the most part, Nanny didn't see what Sitty was doing to us. Nanny's cancer returned.

Sitty still sent me to school with gauze tapered on my forehead and an ace bandage wrapped around my entire head. It wasn't a pretty sight; if only I would have just listened and put on that ugly ass dress. I remember being at school embarrassed and every time someone asked me about it, there was this huge knot in the back of my throat. I wanted to cry, and when I thought no one was looking, tears just streamed down my face but no noise came from my mouth. I couldn't let anyone see me cry because I felt no one cared about me. I knew it wasn't going to change anything. If the school called home, I would just get in more trouble when I got home.

I remember coming home from school and not knowing the teacher had called home telling Sitty I didn't return a math test that needed a parent's signature because I failed it. Sitty filled a mop bucket up with straight bleach, made me get down on my knees with a towel and mop up the floor probably about five times. I could remember the bleach, it burned through my pants, literally ate the skin on my knees, fingers, and elbows until I was bleeding. It felt like millions of needles piercing through every part of me that came into contact with the bleach.

Narrator insert:

It's strange because 37 years later, if I'm not cleaning with bleach, then I feel like whatever I'm cleaning isn't clean enough. When I had a home, bleach was a fixture in my home.

Every now and again we would go back to Auburn AL. and transfer out of schools in New Orleans, because Nanny would always go into remission, and she missed my father; we all did. Nanny would try her hardest to tutor me in my math homework and get me ready for future tests, but I was hard of learning, especially when it came to math. I absolutely hated math. It probably had a lot to do with my father being a professor and the way he taught me seemed more complicated than the way the teachers tried to teach me in school. I was always in lala land during school, trying so hard to hide what was going on at home, and blend in. Mentally, I couldn't focus on anything. I walked on eggshells my entire childhood. Little did I know 37 years later, I would realize that I was never meant to blend in. I was in fact special.

My father being a textile engineer and very impatient, taught me or tried to teach me. I would always nod indicating I understood what he was showing me, when in all actuality, I had no earthly idea. I couldn't focus; I was so scared that he would get mad at me. Nanny tried so hard to get me to understand my math homework, and would tell me that, "You better get it before your father gets home." My father was funny when it came to spankings. He wouldn't abuse us physically the most we got from him, was he would chase us around the pool table and he would pop us with a pool stick, or throw a book at us. My father could say shit that would hurt me more than anything. I loved him so much. The last thing I wanted was for him to be disappointed in me. He was my hero. My father would get so mad to the degree that he would say some of the most hateful things. I know he didn't mean most of the things he said. He would say things like, "you're an idiot," or "you're just like your mother." My father had a pool table in his office right across from the couch where he literally worked until he fell asleep. He rarely slept in the bedroom with Nanny. He did everything on his couch—all of his work for the university. He smoked a carton of cigarettes a day—it seemed like—and where he drank probably six pots of coffee a day. When my father picked up a pool stick, we knew to run. I laugh about it now. Then two hours later he would hug me and tell me, "Narcy, you are the smartest girl in the world. You can do anything, and you just need to focus. If he only knew what was really going on behind closed doors, to Lil Elmo and me, I believe things would have been a lot different. We wanted to tell him, but when we would try to, it seemed as if he were too consumed in his work.

Chapter 6

PRINCESS

My aunt, Nanny's sister (we're going to call her Princess), was also my age, so it was always a headache to explain how she was my aunt, when we hung out like friends. I used to beg to spend the night over at Princess's house because she had hundreds of Barbie's and some of the coolest doll houses ever. We always role played. She was always the Princess, and you already know I was the prince. It sucked she would be Ariel and I would be Prince Eric. The princess really thought she could sing (I'm not trying to be ugly), but she sucked. Later on that year I got to go on a cruise with them to the Bahamas and we were supposed to go to Disney World too, but Princess, and I bickered the entire time, and we didn't make it to the Bahamas.

Nanny packed my clothes, and I remember this bright pink jumper with a big bird on it I wore most of the trip, while Princess got to wear short shorts, tank tops—all the cool kids clothes. I stayed embarrassed the entire time. I had my first Andes chocolate and till this day it's my favorite mint. They would leave them on our pillows every morning when they cleaned our rooms. They tasted so good.

Spending the night, and hanging out with Princess came to an end when Princess and I got caught in her kiddie pool humping. Her mom was in the kitchen window. I think she even recorded us. If I remember correctly, she freaked the fuck out; she must have not freaked out that much if she was recording us. Anyways, people are asses. Princess's mother always had something to say about everyone; she was always gossiping. I thought it was ridiculous and I was young. I think Princess's mom kept me around like she did because she wanted the scoop on Sitty husband's ex-wife. It was like she fed off of Sitty's misery, and loved it. I wanted Princess's life, except for her father. I didn't understand why I couldn't have all the things Princess had. Why was I any different? Did I not deserve that life? I didn't understand why my life had to be so unfair, and cruel. It took me 37 years to figure it all out. Princess's dad came to visit us in Auburn; they were in the middle of transitioning to move to Auburn AL. from New Orleans. They were in the process of selling their home, and Nanny's father wanted to be close to her because her health was deteriorating. At this time I was probably 11 years old, and for some reason I had to give my room up to Nanny's father while they were in town, and I refused to, so he and I ended up sharing my room. That didn't last long because I freaked out when he started abusing me, and making me feel extremely uncomfortable. I immediately ran downstairs to tell Nanny. I told her and she immediately smacked me. She said I was a liar, and that her father would never do such a thing. I got in trouble as soon as they left town and returned to New Orleans from their visit with us.

Nanny took me into the guest bathroom in our home and held my hands under scorching hot water until literally I felt like I was dying. Nanny said that I was a nasty little whore, and even if we weren't family, her father wouldn't look at me twice in that way. The pain got so bad. I couldn't even scream anymore; you couldn't hear anything come out of my mouth. I literally peed on myself and was made to clean it up. I had to sit in my pissy clothes 30 minutes before my father arrived home from work so he wouldn't know anything about it, I literally would beg Nanny and Sitty for a second chance, or tell them I wouldn't do it again, even when I did nothing wrong, but there was no sympathy in their eyes, and they never felt bad. They just told me I deserved every treatment I got. At this time, I knew Nanny's medication had gotten the best of her, and she sought higher doses. The pain was unbearable, which made her an addict. Her behavior became unacceptable, and with age I understood that addiction got the best of her. My father knew nothing about this all along.

Chapter 7

RUN AWAY

I think Sitty was making up rules for the Quran. Our life was a living hell and I believed those rules were not from the Quran. I gave away all my belongings, thinking I could buy friends. It beats Sitty taking them from me, because eventually she would get mad and take the things my father bought me away. I had to wear shorts and shirts in pools and beaches, which we went to on few occasions while my father had work related conventions. One of my favorite beach trips was to Myrtle Beach South Carolina. We would stay at the Embassy Suites and there were literally six buffets filled with anything you could think of. They would make your omelet the way you wanted, and I felt like a queen; the hotel was gorgeous. Lil Elmo had to wear shirts at pools, and beaches which pissed me off because Lil Baghdadi didn't have to. I never understood why. My brother and I really weren't bad kids; but we were considered to be problem kids. Sitty always poked at Lil Elmo for being fat. Nonetheless, I loved my brother no matter what. He was an angry little boy, and 37 years later, I can honestly say that I understand why. My heart breaks for him every day because I can only pray that his soul and spirit finds the peace he truly deserves.

The abuse got so bad I remember Sitty and Nanny telling my brother and me we were going to get it when we got home from school because we would tell my father about them. I got sick of all the shit. I packed a box of things and walked away from the school. One afternoon, when school was closed, instead of catching the bus and going home, I began walking. I thought if I walked long enough, I would be free, and then no one would realize I was gone, and would be left alone. I told my best friend, (we will call her Lola) to run away with me. We planned everything out. She would get her box of favorite things, and I would do the same, and we would escape. I used to talk to Lola about everything that was going on at home. She was so innocent, and I'm sure she didn't understand the extreme of my situation, but she was my best friend, and she was down. We were pretty young, and we thought we were getting somewhere, but we were actually going around the same block over and over again, ending up at Lola's other best friend Jordan's house. We went as far as making up this lie that my dad married Lola's mom and we were sisters. Jordan's mom called the police. My father and my step mom were at the police station waiting on us. I'm pretty sure the police didn't come to hear my reason for running away given the fact that my father was a well-known textile engineer at Auburn University. At that point he was untouchable. I remember returning to school the next day and my punishment for running away was that I had to sit in the library while my classmates went to the zoo. My stepmom called the school and made sure I wasn't included in the field trip. I had to sit in the library.

I also remember all holidays at school being extremely depressing considering we were Muslims, so on every Halloween, Christmas, Easter, while all the other kids got candy and did arts and crafts that were holiday related, I wasn't allowed to partake in the celebrations. I loved being in chorus, and loved singing, just hated not being able to participate. I missed out on Disney trips the school got to go on, and trips to France. I never got to go. I remember all the kids getting ready for these trips. Their parents bought them new swimsuits, and clothes just for the trip. They also got the coolest luggage bags, and they got cell phones, and credit cards. I wouldn't ever imagine getting any of that. I wasn't your average American girl. I was a confused Egyptian for most of my youth, and it took me 37 years to heal, which we will discuss further along.

I made a friend growing up. He was a little like me. He was a Jehovah's witness, and from my understanding they did not celebrate holidays either, and they were strict in their upbringing. He was a kind boy. His name was Evan and from the little that I have seen he's turned out quite alright. He is a decent young man, and I would like to run into him again, and compare stories. I am sure he has some good ones.

Chapter 8

SHORT SHORTS

The principal called home one day to tell my parents that I was wearing too much make up. Little did the principal know I had stolen that make up from Nanny. The principal also told Nanny my locker was stuffed with clothes. The principal had no idea I was planning to run away again. I wanted to wear makeup like all the other girls, and wear short shorts just like them too, but being brought up a Muslim, or honestly any respectful family, you shouldn't wear shorts above the knees, but for women especially in a Muslim home, they couldn't be above the knees. I wasn't allowed to wear tank tops, get my nails done, and none of the normal things, but all the others were doing.

I remember Nanny sewing some shorts up for me, and Sitty in the background saying, "Nanny, I don't even know why you're trying. The fool's going to roll them up anyways when she gets to school." Sitty knew me so well. I sure as hell did, and that morning Sitty warned me, "She said if you come home with creases in your shorts, you're going to wish you never wore them. Man my punishment for that was ridiculous. Sitty took me to the backyard, and at that time we had rabbits. We were mating them, or we would skin them and eat them. Sitty gathered up a handful literally of rabbit shit, the little poops were like little pellets, and made me eat them. I think my father was out of town, because we sat, outside with me bawling for at least four hours. Sitty made sure I ate all of the shit. I mean I was crying so badly, boogers were running into my mouth, and getting everywhere. I never played, or even looked at a rabbit sense, and I sure as hell didn't wear shorts until I finally left home at 16b years old and exploded. We will talk about it later on.

Chapter 9

TRAIN CHOO CHOO

―――――

My father's coping mechanism when he got upset with Nanny and Sitty was to either go into his office at home, and slam the door, or he would pack his stuff and leave for the night, go to a hotel, or just go to his office at the University and sleep. He never stuck around to sort things out. I guess that's how Nanny and Sitty got away with all the things they were doing to us. It didn't make things better for Lil Elmo and me; it made things worse for us because then Sitty and Nanny took their anger out on us.

Narrator Insert:

It has taken me 37 years to realize Nanny felt alone. She needed my father; she needed to be loved the right way, but my father didn't know how. I know it all felt like a slap in the face toward the end of her life. God rest her soul.

I painted a picture of what a good or normal family was supposed to be like, and my family was far from it. It took a lot of healing and understanding for me to get to where I'm in my life right now. I had to accept that people are the way that they are and I can't change them, or make them better than they really are. I allowed people to water me down, and dim my light for so long. I've finally learned that I'm an amazing human being, and God allowed the things to happen in my life to steer me in the right direction and make me stronger. My purpose 37 years later is clear. I'm here to help heal those of you that have given up. I'm going to shine my light and share my love to help bring you out of the dark. I'm a living testimony It's possible.

My father was consumed in his work, and my father got tired. His father passed away when he was a child, so he didn't know how to be the father that we needed at this time in our lives. He came from lack, and tried his hardest to do his best for his family. So when my father left after getting into it with Nanny and Sitty over us, and the way they were mistreating us, we got it handed to us a lot worse. They really hated our guts. I understand now that we all were fighting our own demons, but it hurt knowing the kids suffered because of the adults in our lives.

My father finally got sick of the abuse that was going on at home and he decided he was going to move out and leave Lil Elmo and me with the stepfamily. Eventually, we moved in with him, but it didn't get any better. Everything then was our fault especially when Nanny and my father got to arguing. So now my father had so much anger toward us; it was like a see-saw, no one was ever happy. Sadly, they did nothing to resolve their differences, and reunite to make our lives better. They were selfish, and we didn't matter at this point.

My father was the hardest on Lil Elmo. My father handled our situation the worst way possible. He didn't know how to fix things, and he continued to take his anger out on us, whenever Nanny stressed him out, blowing up his phone, and calling all his family in Egypt begging for their attention. Actually, I knew the family got sick of it, and wished she would just leave them alone. I couldn't imagine being Nanny. Nanny had all these terminal illnesses, had to deal with Sitty, and Sitty was evil, and selfish. Nanny had a husband that was fed up, and had washed his hands clean of both Nanny and Sitty. He loved his kids, but was tired of the shit. Nanny held my father's kids over his head at times to get his attention, and most of the time it worked. You have to think one man has to support six kids—a quarter of a million dollar home—take care of his family in Egypt, deal with a crazy ass mother in law, make sure all of us are in sports and dance, piano classes, etc… That's a lot for one man, especially when you add in your wife is terminally ill, and the entire family doesn't understand how to communicate, and work together. It's tough.

Narrator insert:

I have learned that I took after Nanny. I would go to the extremes to get my boyfriend's attention. I mean I would go so far to the point that their entire families lost respect for me, and wished their sons would leave my crazy ass. Hell! I took after my father as well over the years. I would walk out and avoid any and all altercations in all relationships. I didn't understand what it was to be in a healthy relationship, or what boundaries were. You will see the growth in my life as you continue to read.

From what I was taught, when an Egyptian Muslim girl hits puberty, she gets married off. My father told me that one of his students asked for my hand in marriage, and asked what I thought about it. Sitty was always poking at this man because he was overweight, but no one knew him like I did. He was extremely quiet, and he was just in the States on a school visa from Egypt, and was studying and hoped to stay in the States when he graduated. By this time, Lil Elmo and I were living in an apartment complex in downtown Auburn with my father. We were allowed to do whatever we wanted because my father was always at work, and after dealing with the shit we had dealt with all our childhood, we did that exactly. Well, this man that asked my father for my hand in marriage, I didn't take it seriously, and at this time, I was probably 15 years old and had just started exploring, and trying to do what all the other girls were doing. This student who wanted to marry me did absolutely anything I asked him to do, and I didn't care for him. I took advantage of his kindness, and now realized at the time, I didn't deserve a good man like him. God had better plans for him, and he ended up traveling the world. I tried messaging him on Facebook a few months ago to apologize and all he said was, "Don't ever contact me again." I deserved it.

I messaged him one year right after he asked for my hand in marriage. It was right at Valentine's day and I told him I had never received a Valentine from anyone, and within the hour, he brought me a dozen roses and a huge box of chocolates. I didn't know how to genuinely be thankful. It was just something free. This man wasn't the only man my parents tried to set me up with. There was this other guy from Egypt who sold African American makeup. The whole family met him at Golden Corral and I was Just 16 years old with Dreadlocks. I remember Nanny taking a dog brush to my hair in the shower. She cut the ponytail off, and in her exact words, she said, "No daughter of mine will have nasty hair!" She literally started combing them out. They were new so it wasn't too hard. Then she covered my hair with a hijab (Muslim scarf), and took me to meet this man. We both sat at our own table and I thought this man was hideous. I told him I was gay. So…Yeah I got an ass whooping of a lifetime. (I took that beating like a champion. I mean I was Mohammed Ali). That put a hold on my parents trying to marry me off for a while. Thank God.

A little off topic. Anyways I'm not sure how or why my father left me at the apartment at 16 years old and left for Egypt with my brother, but he did, and I was left alone all summer. With that freedom, there came hell… literally…hell… I learned a lot of things a 16 year old should have never learned: thunderbird (Cheap wine that fucked you up), cocaine, pot , alcohol, GHb—what it meant to have the train ran on you, and rape. I was literally riding around in a Cadillac in my 22's with a group of older people who at the time I thought cared for me. This was my first encounter with GHB, (P. is what I'll call him). He was in JROTC with my older brother. Now he's an ex-army veteran. Every time I see him since then it puts this fear in my soul each time we cross paths, because he took part in a gangbang with four other black guys in my father's apartment. This all occurred when my father was away in Egypt.

This group of young men put GHB in my drink. Every time I went to take a shot of crown royal, everyone would shout out, "You didn't take a shot." This was on one evening when all of us were hanging out at my father's apartment. We were playing spades, smoking blunts, and getting drunk. I was new to all of this. I was naive, and trusted everyone back then, to the point of me putting myself in situations like these, and ended up in me learning the hard way. Peer pressure was a bitch. I would take another shot, just to be on their "level." These people knew what they were doing the entire time. The last thing I could remember was someone banging on my apartment door, sounding like they were the cops. I was naked passed out on the carpet in the same spot Lil Elmo and I always "wrestled" (so many bad memories).

My neighbor was banging on the door while yelling, "Get your clothes on, you're coming with me to get a shower. They ran a train on you!! P is bragging about it, telling everyone! " I didn't know what the hell a train was. That was when I got my first STD (Chlamydia). I could remember itching and burning every time I went to pee, and then my privates started to have an odor. It got unbearable, so I went to the emergency room, and was treated.

Narrator insert:

I made it out alive. I'm thankful that I wasn't killed. God had me without a doubt. I have met people out here in these streets that had sex and literally contracted HIV the first time. I encourage you to always wear protection, and quit drinking if you know you can't have more than one drink.

The woman that came and got me from my apartment ended up dying five years later from heart problems. I didn't know what the train was until this unfortunate event. It's crazy because when I was living in Alabama, I would run into P at the dollar general, and his buddy that took part in it, and they would say, "What's up Narcy," as if we were supposed to be cool. Little did they know or even could ever care that this event really traumatized me, and ruined many years of my life. I know God has a special place for people like this, and I found it in my heart many years later to forgive not them, but for my peace.

Chapter 10

SUICIDE ATTEMPT

My aunt came down to go to school for a little while from Dubai, and I ended up living with her and my cousin for a little while. I remember wanting attention so bad, I lied that I took 40 aspirins when all I really took was five. I played sick, and my aunt rushed me to the emergency room, where I acted as if I were a threat to myself. They put me in the kids unit so they could keep an eye on me. I am pretty sure at this time my father was always working and I missed him. I remember him bringing me a rose, in a glass vase and they wouldn't let me have it because the vase was glass. I know I gave my poor aunt hell. She barely spoke English, but you knew when this woman was mad, her Russian or Arabic would scare the shit out of me.

The first time I ever got high was when I lived with her. I had smoked pot with this hippie that all my classmates crushed on, and would go and buy drugs from this guy when they got out of school. His house was the party house everyone liked going to. I thought it would be cool to get high because everyone around me was getting high. I couldn't hide my bloody red eyes for anything. My aunt could smell the marijuana on me, and she was determined to teach me a lesson. She called the police on me, and I was scared to death—that taught me a lesson alright. I was upset with my aunt to the point that I ran her back to Dubai. My father pretty much pawned me off on my poor aunt, and she got tired of dealing with my ungrateful ass. I didn't have the proper training I needed to be a well-mannered teen. I know she feared I would corrupt my cousin, Dahlula. Moreover, she missed my uncle back in Dubai. He could blame her for her actions.

Chapter 11

KITTY

I met a girl in high school. We called her Kitty (she loved cats). I told her about everything that was going on in my life, and she went and told her mother. I'm sure they felt sorry for me, because soon after, her mom decided to get involved and asked my father to adopt me. He was more than willing. I knew it hurt him, because all I can remember was him walking toward the podium in court. He signed his rights over, and with his head down he exited the courtroom, and not once did he look at me. I know he felt as if he let me down, and I know he was sorry. He tried as best as he knew how to. I was hurt, but strangely and quickly I brushed it under the rug just like I had done with everything else that hurt me in my life growing up. I was beginning to become immune to this type of hurt.

Kitty's life was the American life I thought I wanted. Her mom was always at work, and we were left really to do whatever we wanted. I considered kitty a hippy, and I loved dragging along with her because she hung out with all the hot hippies, and the skateboard dudes. Kitty and her family would go to Knoxville Tennessee oftentimes and leave me behind. I took advantage of it. I remember going out with a couple so called friends, and back then I thought I was the life of the party. I literally brought home the entire bar. I mean there were cars parked all up and down her street into her driveway. People brought their own alcohol. The next morning I found people passed out outside, on top of the washer and dryer in the living room in kitty's parents bed.. Kitty, if you're reading this right now, I am so sorry. To this day I still don't get how kitty's parents never found out. Not a trace of the party was in sight.

I had a boyfriend at the time that I would call Cracker. Remember I was 16 years old then. The two of us lied to kitty's mom and told her cracker was 19 when really I think he was in his late 20's. I did a lot of things that I am not proud of during the few years I lived with these great people. I remember Cracker and I stealing Kitty's mom and stepdad's CD's and Dvd's, and pawning them at Hastings, because cracker, and I wanted to get some cocaine. Cracker was older and took advantage of the fact that I had to be home at a certain time every night, so he was constantly cheating. At this point I still had no idea what love really was. I know there were times we weren't together and I would go and have intimacy with other people and the next day, we would argue because I supposedly cheated on him—when really I had blacked out and I was taken advantage of. He acted like he cared, but he was the type of guy to run and laugh about it all to his homies. I ended up trying shrooms for the first time at Kitty's house, in her front yard. I remember connecting my friends freckles on his face.

Personally, it looked like he was wearing a full body armor, and Kitty it was hilarious, I would psst as if I were trying to get a cat to come my way to her. I really thought she was a cat. It was an experience. I still wouldn't change it for the world. While living with Kitty's family, one of my very first jobs was at Kroger. While employed at Kroger, I met this chick from Columbus Georgia. Her name was Shana.

Shanna always bragged about how much more money she would make when she lived in Columbus Georgia. I should have asked her what the hell she was doing in Alabama, if it was so good in Georgia. Shanna ended up convincing me into moving with her to Georgia—one of the worst mistakes of my life. Kitty's mom let me take all my bedroom furniture and helped me move everything to Columbus Ga. I think about that time, she was sick of my shit, that was becoming a trend in my life at this time. I was one tough act to follow, and I sure as hell was a hard pill to swallow.

Chapter 12

GEORGIA

Well, I was finally in Georgia. I had no job, no car, and Shanne was at work, so getting a cigarette was almost impossible until one day. I was sitting outside on our porch and I saw this sexy blonde beach bum looking dude washing his white Acura shirt. I stroll over to bum a smoke, and he asked me what kind I smoke. I told him menthol, and he said he had a friend that smokes menthol and was coming over He asked me to sit for a few minutes and he should be pulling up. We're going to call his buddy D.J. When he finally pulled up, I was invited inside Beach Bum's house, and on this dresser, I saw piles of this crystal looking substance. Beach Bum asked me if I had ever smoke, and I lied because all I wanted to do was fit in. This was the worst lie of my life thus far, and I joke around about it now. It was the worst cigarette I had ever bummed in my life. At first beach, Bum wouldn't let me smoke it. He said that's how people got addicted to it, and he had been smoking the shit for 13 years prior to meeting me. Beach Bum had the house, friends, car, and family that I wanted my entire life—that's what I pictured a proper boyfriend relationship should consist of. I still lived in my apartment across the street but it got to the point where he didn't want me to leave there, so I ended up moving in with him. That Disneyland phase ended quickly. Oh my GOD! The shit we put each other through; I mean I thought it was love. I remember him leaving me lines on the dresser each morning when he left for work. I guess that's what kept me there. I was new to Methamphetamine. I remember freaking out whenever he left. I thought him and his friends were outside talking shit about me, when he wasn't even home. I thought he was screwing, "Dope dealer." She was a bad ass, I thought. Everyone loved her, not until many years later did I understand why Dope dealers are worshiped by dope heads. I used to be one. I should know.

I'm just glad that lifestyle is over. I literally saw pink monkeys in the trees, while I was sweeping our front porch at 3 a.m. I had to learn the high and what the effects on me were the hard way, because I thought I wanted to be a part of Beach Bum's lifestyle at the time. I just wanted to fit in. We all see where that got me. It only gets crazier. I should have never lied and said I knew what that crystal looking substance was on Beach Bum's dresser. It was definitely one of the worst lies I ever told that affected a major part of my life, but God knew what he was doing. It took me many years later to realize why Beach Bum wasn't ever around. Besides the fact that I was crazy as hell on that ash and he didn't want to be around me. Crystal meth is a drug I learned he chased all the time because ten years later I did the same thing. I had to learn for myself. If Beach Bum wasn't figuring out ways to get money to buy more dope, or selling it off somewhere, smoking with other people that's what that lifestyle does; it alienates you from society, from anything healthy, and your family especially. It turns you into a soulless person. You forget how to care for anyone. You easily lose yourself.

Beach bum put a stop to me going anywhere with him because I embarrassed him so many times in front of his friends and threatened to call the cops on everyone. Hell! I was young, and didn't know how to control my high. I didn't think anything was wrong with me; I thought it was everyone else's fault.

Beach bum got out there a few times himself. I remember him getting so paranoid thinking the cops were after him, and he made me take his truck and drive it back home to Alabama. He thought I was going to listen and go to Alabama, but I didn't. He wrote a letter saying that the truck he was going to make me leave belonged to him, and if anything was found such as paraphernalia or drugs, it was also his. He was so paranoid he thought the cops were going to run up in our home any minute. He wanted to protect me. I left but I didn't go back to Alabama. He made it clear in the letter he made me take that whatever trouble he was in I had nothing to do with it. I ended up getting drunk, and somehow or another I ended up at some guy's house and got up the next morning not sure about what had happened but made it back to Beach Bum's house. Beach Bum was still hiding out with his Dope dealer. He ended up coming home later the next morning, immediately got in my face, and shoved me to the ground, and drug me by my legs to the side of the road. He told me I was trash, and called me every name in the book. Alcohol was never a friend of mine. This was my second run in with GHB. I was drugged, and everyday living in that neighborhood was hell. I was reminded by people. I guess I was so drunk I couldn't recognize them, Any time I saw them on the street and they approached me bringing up this incident, I looked dumbfounded, and I was embarrassed. Beach Bum later realized I was raped, and wanted to kill everyone on that block. The Dope dealer spread the rumor that Beach Bum and I had HIV to this day and I still question why she and I had beef. Man dope will make you a monster. Being raped started to become normal to me; it didn't even phase me like it would most females. I never got emotional about it, so there wasn't much I got emotional about. Before too long I got used to Beach Bum leaving me alone at the house for three days at a time, with no power, or dope, and absolutely no food. I ended up meeting the neighbors that moved into my old place, the palace right across the street from Beach Bum's house. The house Shanna and I rented right when we moved from Alabama—the same house I lived in when I met Beach Bum.

Chapter 13

HIS BOYS

On occasion Beach Bum would leave me at home without food, dope, hope, power, the water worked. In the beginning of our relationship our home on 18th, the street was set up like a college student's duplex. He was attending school at the time, but it didn't last. His father had a bunch of rental property and gave him this house. Beach Bum would do the maintenance of all the other property and his father would let him work his rent off. He was a momma's boy, and his father adored the hell out of him. He was a loveable guy, but when meth was in the picture, he wasn't the Beach Bum his parents knew, or anyone knew for that matter. We managed to wreck his house. I would get so geeked up, and paint every room of the house a different color every day. I wouldn't paint it the right way; I would put layer on layer. Beach Bum was a painter by occupation. When he left me at the house for days at a time, I had to resort to finding my own food, and reaching out to neighbors for help.

In the old apartment that Shanna and I moved into right across the street when we moved out, a guy moved in. We would call him Peter P. He worked in a cafeteria and would bring food home every night. I made sure I walked my strung out ass across the street to eat. I would say Peter P felt sorry for me. There were things about this man I didn't know, and you will learn soon. Things that happened in this home, I thought only happened in the movies. Thanks Peter P for feeding me for all the years that you did, and showing me things that really happen in the real world. You taught me a lot, by no means am I trying to put your business out there. I just hope people learn from our experiences. Looking back and realizing if I were at my best in my life, I would never have associated with anyone, but God knew I was extremely hard headed and made my life unmanageable until I straightened the hell up.

I learned quickly that Peter P was gay, and I would never have known if it weren't for the times I would come over and try to hang out. He wouldn't let me hang out for too long; he was quick to run me off. If it weren't for these select two young white boys that would always come around when they were broke, and didn't have money, Peter P would get them high or drunk, and he would take advantage of them. These guys were straight as a board until they were under the influence. When it would just be Peter P. and me and he would be tipsy and I would be sipping on a beer, we would get to talking, and he would start telling me all the fucked up stories between them. It got to the point that he would get jealous of me because he thought I wanted his boys. All I wanted to do was eat his food. Later on in life, I did end up hooking up with two of his boys. I was so intoxicated and it didn't make any sense. I didn't care about myself. You could tell when Peter P. would get jealous when I was around these guys. This man would snap and it would come out of nowhere, just because the guys gave me all their attention. I honestly at that time could care less about any man, I just wanted to be high or drunk.

Chapter 14

PROSTITUTION

———

Whenever Peter Piper would run me off, I would run to another so called friend, who acted like he had my best interest but in actuality all he wanted to do was fuck me. We're going to call him Whitie. He was the blackest in color black man you would ever see, but he acted the whitest, and yes I'm stereotyping. I'm really just trying to get you to see the picture. He got me into prostitution, and I had easy money.

He lived in Columbus Ga., rode his cab all through the military base, and had access to all the horny young guys in the military, and multi-million dollar married men who would have lost everything if their family found out. These young guys didn't know how to talk to a woman, and these guys would quickly pay for a prostitute. I met Whitie while I worked at a bar downtown Columbus Ga. In the beginning, I was freaked out about it, but when you're under the influence of many different drugs and alcohol and you have been up delirious for days, you tend to lose the little dignity you have, and just don't give a fuck. Whitie would drop me off at the hotel, with another prostitute and we would literally go in a room, lay down for less than ten minutes, and the guys would cum. You could tell they weren't getting any, and we would make over 1,000.00 dollars a night. They also bought all the drugs and alcohol we wanted.

I met one man who wasn't military. He owned his own construction business, had a beautiful family at home, but enjoyed cocaine, probably more than he enjoyed his family. God bless his heart; he couldn't get hard for the life of him when he did cocaine. I couldn't understand why this idiot would do this shit to himself, until now and I look back and see I was also an idiot.

It would take me and three other girls to entertain this dummy and he would literally be so embarrassed that he couldn't get hard. He would be throwing hundred dollar bills at us every time we looked at him. I entertained him once, hung out in the room for 20 minutes and got 800.00 dollars and took off. I never stuck around to risk the chance of police showing up. I was always careful. This guy bought a few of the girls' cars, and set them up in their own houses. I was never bold enough to stick around for any of that. The inevitable happened a few years later. This man ended up losing his business, going bankrupt; he lost everything.

Every time I got Whitie to scoop me up, it would be because I was starving, and knew he would feed me, and it made time pass, which was better than sitting at home waiting for Beach Bum to get home. I never knew when that would be. So I never gave Whitie the time to get me for too long and have a chance to have sex with me… I always rushed to get back to Beach Bum's house so that I could get high hopefully. Whitie always told me that he would take care of me if I would just leave Beach Bum, but little did I know by this time Crystal Meth controlled me, and I was codependent on what I thought was Beach Bum, but in fact it was the dope.

Beach Bum and I would get into some of the ugliest arguments. I would call his mom and tell her everything that we were doing. I didn't care who I hurt in the process. He was a momma's boy so everything I would say to her went in one ear and out the other. His mother would just blame everything on me, and tell Beach Bum to get rid of me. He wouldn't have these problems anymore. I honestly don't think I would have stuck around as long as I did if it weren't for the dope. By this time Beach Bum managed to make me feel like no one else would ever want me.

Beach Bum and I would get so high, and he would take things apart and never put them back together. This man had so many projects going on at one time. It started to look like a hoarder's house. He would take motors out of anything with a motor and make sex toys to use with me, as he played a porno for us to watch. Our relationship got so bad; we weren't civil to each other, except for when he wanted to have sex; he was nice to me for those few minutes, and I ate it up. He made sure he had dope, as we were fucking, and made me feel like a dope. However, I later realized I had become one, because I only thought about being dope, and how I would get high. It was like my soul left my body, and nothing else mattered. It was an empty feeling.

I remember one day he sent me to pick up Chinese food, and he wanted Mongolian beef. The sign on the buffet read Mongolian beef. When I got home, he took the carry out box full of food and smashed it in my face. Then he started beating me. Now that I'm older and have experienced it full force, I know he didn't mean to be the way that dope made him, and he may not know it but I forgive him.

I used to be Beach Bum's look out when we would go and steal shit. When the cops were pulling up, I would give him a heads up. We were back behind Kmart one night, and he broke into their shed. We ended up stealing 13 brand new lawn mowers, and selling them for dope. I ran into a nice hotel with him and stole a flat screen TV, and sold that for dope too. I am not proud of any of these. It's a lesson learned, and since I've done it, I hope you don't.

Narrator Insert:

I am sharing these stories with you because I want you to not have to go through the things I went through. Not many of us are as blessed as I am. I made it out alive. If you can read my book and learn from it, you can make it through anything.

Chapter 15

SNITCH

This coward wore a wire in our home. This guy was supposed to be one of Beach Bum's friends. He was more than a friend; he was like a brother. They grew up together. This guy whom we will call, Quick, set up the Dope dealer. I can't remember how exactly we found out, but Beach Bum turned around and went to Quick's house and stole four wheelers, and a bunch of other shit—when he knew Quick would be out of town. Beach Bum got his revenge. He was loyal to the game, and when he called you his friend, you really were his friend. A lot of users, and so called friends back then took advantage of Beach Bum's loyalty. Beach bum is clean now and raising our beautiful daughter. We will call her Angel. I'll talk more about her later on.

A week later, Quick and his brother came by our house while Beach Bum was gone. I saw them from the window walked around back trying to look in our backyard. This was the first time I really crossed the line, and honestly to this day, I regret the hell out of it. Beach Bum had been gone a few days. I was starving and going through withdrawals bad. Beach Bum and I were not on good terms. I told Quick what Beach Bum had done. I betrayed Beach Bum. I haven't had the courage to actually own up to it.

Narrator insert:

Beach Bum, I betrayed you. I take responsibility for it; our relationship was so dysfunctional. God knew what he was doing. You have become a wonderful man, and so have I, a wonderful woman. I'm proud of you. Crystal Meth will destroy everyone and anything that comes in its path.

Chapter 16

DISOWNED

My relationship with Beach Bum got unbearable. I moved out, and moved back to Auburn AL. Shortly after I found out I was pregnant I told my brother, Lil Elmo. I thought I could confide in him, and he would keep it a secret at least until I was ready to share this information with my family. I was already disconnected from the family, and I just wanted my father to smile when he saw me, and we could try to have one decent conversation, and talk about life for once. I missed my father. Lil Elmo wasn't having that; he ran to my father quickly and told him. What brother would want to go out of his way to cross his little sister that did nothing to him her entire life but showed him love? My brother failed to realize telling my father the way that he did, caused my father literally to disown me. It didn't bring my brother and my father closer together.

I could remember telling Nanny about it. She was pretty much living her last days and she rubbed my belly, and told me she couldn't wait to meet the baby Angel. Nanny apologized to me for the pain she caused me and Lil Elmo growing up. I forgave her. I loved her. There were great times, and the great times, I would like to think the good outweighed the bad. Not even a week later my father called me to tell me that Nanny passed away. I forgave her; she deserved my forgiveness. Her life wasn't easy either.

I pray that Lil Elmo gets right with himself, and is at peace when he leaves this world, because honestly, we have been through hell, and really need out. I forgive my brother, but this wouldn't be the only time he would screw me over. Years later, he took my inheritance after the death of my father. My brother is a scam, and I can finally admit it to myself, and quit defending him because he has never defended me. I forgive him, and will always love him from a distance, but I will leave it at that.

Chapter 17

ABORTION

I remember calling Beach Bum from Auburn to tell him I was pregnant, and he was so excited. I returned to Columbus Ga. thinking Beach Bum and I were going to live happily ever after. I was wrong. I ended up moving into a duplex with the help of Kitty's family. I started working in Downtown Columbus. I was a fixture at a pizza joint. Everyone knew and loved me. I was that pregnant girl that worked full time. I was still using dope in the beginning of my pregnancy. Beach Bum didn't know at first. Then it started to get hard pretending to be sober, but I somehow got away with it, probably because Beach Bum was always geeked up, or he was always gone. I think I was six months pregnant and Beach Bum and his family talked me into moving back into their home. Little did I know Beach Bum's mom had scheduled an abortion appointment for me, and I was told the night before I was scheduled to get an abortion. I told Beach Bum I wouldn't do it. He got so mad he flipped the bedroom mattress and box spring on top of me and started kicking the shit out of it. I knew the drugs, and his parents had a lot to do with his actions. As I said, when I called him to inform him I was pregnant from Alabama, Beach Bum was thrilled. Afterwards, I kept begging him and telling him I wanted to keep my baby, and he continued to beat the shit out of me.

I managed to get away. I ran out of the front door, barefoot all the way to the emergency room, while crying and scared to death. I knew that if I didn't get away, Beach Bum would have done something he would have never been able to recover from; it would have ruined his life. I ended up at the emergency room, and I can remember how cold I was, and how neglected and worthless I felt. Beach Bum's family just gave me confirmation, that I was alone, and no one really gave a fuck. The next morning, the staff at the hospital put me in a women's shelter. During this time, I was told that if I was associated with Beach Bum, I would get kicked out of the shelter. I ended up moving back into Beach Bum's house because I didn't like the rules at the shelter, and at the time, I loved him, even after what he did to me. No matter what people do to me, I forgive them, and always give them the benefit of the doubt. We returned to our usual daily lives. I would be left at home, as Beach Bum ran the streets and left me home alone.

I got the phone call, and we all knew Nanny's final days were nearing. My dad called me to tell me. I tried calling Beach Bum to see if he would drive me to Auburn Al. to see Nanny before she passed away, but I couldn't reach him. So Whitie ended up driving me in his taxi cab. I saw my step mom lying in the hospital bed, with her face sunk in, as well as her eyes. I'll never forget the way she looked. Nanny put her hand on my belly and said, "I can't wait to meet baby Angel; she is going to be as strong and beautiful as her momma." This was the first time my Momma apologized to me. I forgave her and told her I knew now that it was her sickness and all the medication that made her act the way she did.

One week before Angel was born, Nanny passed away. God rest her soul. I remember after giving birth to Angel, Beach Bum and I were still using drugs in our home. We had the house separated so it was actually a duplex, and I couldn't wait till Angel was asleep so I could run over to the other side of the house and get high. Now that' I'm sober, I regret my actions and just want to tell my daughter that I'm sorry. I know I could have been a better mother. Beach Bum's parents took over raising Angel, and now that I look back at it, it was for the best. Neither of us was good; at the time I had resentment and thought the world was out to get me. Drugs will take you out of reality and put you in an extremely dark place. Thank God she was brought up by his parents because she is a very beautiful young lady. I eventually moved out of Beach Bum's house, and lived across the street with Peter P. for a hot minute. Beach Bum and I continued trying to work things out, while our daughter lived with his parents. I remember Beach Bum's dad in his wheelchair with Angel in his lap wherever he went; she was his little partner.

While I lived at Peter P. house, I'm not even going to lie. I stayed high or drunk. Angel never crossed my mind. I was extremely selfish, and I sincerely regret it very much.

Chapter 18

JUMP OUT BOYS

▬▬▬

I remember one evening I was on the phone with Beach Bum talking about coming over to talk, and see if we can work things out, but clearly I knew all he wanted to do was get laid, because when you're under the influence of crystal meth, it's like your soul isn't even there. We honestly didn't know what we were doing. Well, I looked out of my window at Peter P's house, and all I saw were cops blocking off the road in front and behind our street and a big white van pulled up. This was my first encounter with the jump out boys; well, not mine exactly.

They had this huge Ram. They used to force the doors down at Beach Bum's house. I ran across the street and I screamed out, "What are y'all doing!" And the officer asked,

"Are you coming over here to tell us something we need to know?" Then I said, "No!" Then the officer said, "Well, then get yourself the fuck away from here."

I watched them bring Beach Bum outside in handcuffs and it hurt watching this. I swear to you, Beach Bum thought for the longest time I had set him up, because literally, we were on the phone together not even five minutes before the jump out boys showed up, but I had nothing to do with his arrest. I ended up seeing Beach Bum swing by his house the next day; he was bonded out and sent to rehab; he ended up going to Bradford. He got out of his parents' van the day after he was bonded out before going to rehab, looked at me, shook his head then got back in the van, after he picked a few things up from his house. I never snitched him out to the police. I wouldn't ever do that. I did rat him out to Quick, and his brother, but never the police. I was under the influence and life was unmanageable. When Beach Bum was off at treatment at Bradford, his family convinced me to move into their home. It was a bummer no one ever asked me if I wanted to go to rehab. Lord knows I needed it just as bad. I'm sure things would have turned out a lot different, but God had better plans, and you will see as you continue reading.

I recall Beach Bum calling us while in rehab and talking to him. It was the sweetest tone and conversation he and I had ever had. Mind you Beach Bum had been using meth 13 years prior to his arrest, so our conversation was a little loopy. He promised to marry me, and we had just had angel. He was already talking about having another child. I'll admit I missed the hell out of him. I know I loved him, and will always love him, but I moved on eventually. It took me many years.

I was working at the time, and Beach Bum made it out of Rehab and was home. He was doing really well going to NA meetings, but I never went to rehab. I guess they thought I was just going to quit, or maybe Beach Bum's mom knew I wasn't going to quit. Perhaps that was why I wasn't offered rehab, and she really wanted to get rid of me. No one was ever good enough for her son. At work I made friends with a cocaine dealer, and I waited tables so I always had cash. I couldn't ask any of Beach Bum's friends for meth, that being my drug of choice at the time, because then Beach Bum would find out. So I resorted to cocaine. My dealer would front me a 40 sack every day, so I always owed him. Shit hit the fan when one day I was at work, and Beach Bum's mom went through my daughter's sock drawer and found all the empty baggies. Beach Bum ended up taking me to work one night, hitting me the whole way to work and spit on me as I was exiting his car. He beat me badly. I was so embarrassed walking into work. Everyone told me not to go back. I linked up with a guy and went on this week straight binge on cocaine, alcohol, you name it. I didn't understand then, but I understand now. God didn't let Beach Bum's mom give me my daughter when I tried to pick her up and leave with her, because she knew I was not right or able to care for her properly. I resented Beach Bum's family for a very long time. I forgive them now. I know for me not going along with the abortion, it saved Beach Bum's life and he learned how to truly love someone—that person being his beautiful daughter. Everything happens for a reason. I forgive them, and I know Beach Bum's momma absolutely adores Angel. They are lucky to have each other. There's a part of me that wished things were different but then I wouldn't be where I'm today and neither would they. I can't understand why my family couldn't stick it out with me through the bad and the good, and get me help like Beach Bum's family did.

Now I understand I really never had a family. I wish that both of my kids have families that are strong, and stick together no matter what. That's what's wrong with this world today. Where is the love?

Chapter 19

DIAMANTE

While living with Peter, I met Diamante. He was a full blown alcoholic. Crystal meth was scarce and alcohol was legal so I turned into a full blown alcoholic too. One extreme to the next, Diamante was always in and out of jail. Whenever he drank, he literally went out of his way to fight anyone, and anything. I gave birth to our son, Trex, and had no one at the hospital with me. It sucked because I didn't' know how I was going to leave the hospital, without a car seat and without a ride. Luckily, my boss bought me one, and Whitie gave me a ride home. I ended up texting Diamante's mother, sending her a picture of our baby and she said the baby was cute and all but I should know it's not her son's because it was black. It broke my heart because God knew my child wasn't black. I had written Diamante while he was incarcerated telling him that I cheated on him with a black guy, and our relationship went downhill from there. It wasn't a good relationship anyways considering it revolved around alcohol, and we were hardly ever sober, so the couple of years we were together, I can't recall any memories. It's all a figment of alcohol; it is what it seems like. The devil is what I would call it. He was abusive. I remember the neighbors called the cops on us one time, and we lied and told the cops we were having rough sex, when really we were fighting like cats and dogs. Another incident, both of us ended up going to jail for wasting the cops time. Neither one of us wanted to admit we were beating each other up. I couldn't see him go to jail again. When Diamante got drunk, the alcohol consumed every ounce of both of us.

Chapter 20

INSIDE JOB

━━━━━━━

I managed to move back to Auburn, Alabama, and put up a defense that I was sober and didn't have an addiction problem, until one day I walk up the road to pick a pack of smokes up drunk. I left Trex in our apartment alone. I thought I would be back before he woke up, only to wake up in a holding cell not understanding why the fuck I was in there. The cops said the only thing that would come out of my mouth was, "Go to my apartment, my baby is there home alone." I was so drunk I couldn't even remember what had happened.

My son was put in foster care. My family didn't care to intervene and help, and they had the opportunity to foster my son, but couldn't care less about our situation. My father's colleague and his family ended up fostering my son. I did everything in my power and got my son back, even the authorities of Alabama said they had never seen someone so determined. I fought for my son.

I remember working at the bowling alley one night, and my boss running up to tell me that I needed to run home. Something was going on with my brother. It was on the news. I looked up at our flat screen TV and the subtitles read, "Terroristic threats made by man and ten hour police standoff." I run to the scene and instantly I called Lil Baghdadi. Surprisingly, he answered, and said, "Narcy, I got this; take care of Trex, and I love you guys." He told me that if he ended up dead I should just know he didn't do it. My brother was found one day before he was supposed to be released hanging in his cell. Supposedly, his cell was cracked open 15 minutes prior to anyone checking on him. Tell me that wasn't an inside job. Look me in my eyes and tell me it wasn't. I promise, no soul will do that.

Living in good Ole, Alabama, where racism is still alive, they were quick to say my brother was shouting out terroristic threats, and made him out to be an animal. When in fact the people that really knew him respected this young man and Lil Baghdadi did everything and anything for anyone. He literally would give you the shoes off of his feet.

Explain to me why the few guys got busted in an incident before this one involving my brother and the family's son that now has custody of my son, unjustly, and illegally. We will soon get into the corruption and the truth behind Lee county Alabama. The incident involved these men transporting illegal drugs to and from Columbia, resulting in a pilot snitching them out, which my brother took the blame for the rest of these straight low life cowards. Now my brother is dead and these idiots are still alive, living their lives with beautiful kids, and families. My brother had to die to allow these morons to live lavishly. The women's family that has dangled my son over my head since he was two, didn't take on the responsibility of raising my son out of the good in their hearts; it was out of the guilt for the truth only they will really ever know involving my brother. My brother deserved justice. Can someone tell me why my brother's death was not investigated, and why when you go to pull records, none are anywhere to be found? How can you take a case and brush it under the rug? Just because someone is an Egyptian, and has an Arabic name doesn't make him a terrorist. It's so unreal how far Alabama took it with the lies they told to cover the idiots.

My brother's death caused a relapse, and the people regained custody of my son. I'm going to make this clear and it's all facts. If you are an Alumni, work for the university, and ex-cop (The family that has custody of my son's husband is, and he's an alcoholic who's relapsed a few times), your kids are in school and go to church with the judges kids, which this family's kids did. The judge, no matter what's really going on chooses to side with them, no matter what it's sickening. Family court is a scam. Literally, they take your kids away from you; put them in homes, allow you to be alienated, when in the court documents it states at least one visit a month. I was alienated since April 14, 2021. It is 2023, and they don't give a damn.

At the end of the day your kids are parroting what the new families have made them believe because they have no choice. Your kids see how powerful these people are, and don't want to piss them off because at the end of the day that is how these kids are going to be fed, and that is where they would have to lay their heads at night. It's sad; the parents aren't given the chance to step in and protect their name to their children. It doesn't help that some of us parents will forever be judged by our past. The system is lazy. Whenever they feel like it, it is when they take your kids away from you, and illegally strip you from your rights and still expect you to pay child support—when they don't even allow you to see your kids.

Chapter 21

R.A.D.S
(Reactive attachment disorder)

After many years of active alcoholism and drug abuse, I still made attempts to call the other family to see how my son was doing. I was still getting blown off, and I can understand now that I wasn't going to be the mother my son needed me to be at the time. God knew it; I didn't. Alcohol always got me in my feelings, and I would call everyone drunk. I'm so glad I am sober now, and we don't have the issue anymore.

The family finally answered my phone call, and asked me if I was ready to be a mother again, and I was excited to say yes. I was living out of a motel in Opelika, the cheapest one for that matter. Drugs came in and out of the place all the time. The family didn't seem to care. I was working at the Huddle house. Some days I would cook, and wouldn't have the money to pay for my room, so I would prostitute, and on other days I made tips and could pay for my room. I met this Marine. We won't go into too much detail about him. He was just a dude that used his wife's credit card to pay for my room bills, and wouldn't leave. So I used him for what he was worth. He invaded my life, so I invaded his resources, and I was straight forward the entire time with him. I never loved him. He was weird. He couldn't kiss and he made weird animal noises when we had sex. I was under the influence, and he had money, so I didn't care. If he was going to use me to make his ex-jealous, then I was going to use him to survive. He ended up being a little bitch at the end. Ugh, I hated even thinking about his dumb ass.

The other family never asked me if I was on drugs, or still drinking; they didn't care to know who my "so-called boyfriend was." They just really wanted me to take my son off their hands, and it confused the fuck out of me. They alienated him from me for years, and then all of a sudden they were begging me to take my son back. I later found out the man of the house began drinking again, so the woman of the house had enough on her plate as it was. So they started bringing Trex to my room on Fridays, and letting him stay with me until Sunday and then he would have to go back, so that he could attend school. However, it got to the point that we were keeping him throughout the week and we enrolled him in school closer to us and I met with the off and on again family in their living room to sign the custody papers. The marine and I found a trailer and the three of us moved in it. I then found out that before the other family decided to communicate with me regarding my son, my son had ran away from their home, and wasn't found for over an hour. The cops found him walking with a dog four miles away from the home. When they asked him where he was going, he said he was going to find his mom, and that she lived near railroad tracks. I screwed up when I let this woman fool me into agreeing for joint custody with her. I'm not too sure how legato that is, given my son's father was still alive. I was just happy to be getting my son back. I didn't realize how manipulative this individual really was.

This family told the marine (my ex) and me my son was diagnosed with R.A.D.S., and that if he wasn't treated he would become a serial killer. She put the fear of God in us. What made the whole situation strange was I was living out of a hotel. I didn't have a car, and she didn't know my boyfriend, and she never asked me if I was sober. She really didn't care. For some reason she was ready to just be done with my son. She said she feared for her life, even the husband said that he was afraid my son was going to hurt his wife. They had to hide knives, and lighters from my son. They stated he would harm their animals, and not once out of the five years my son lived with me did he ever harm any animals at our house. Something had to have happened for my son to run away like that. There were times my son would visit and he would have bruises on his arms, and he told me Mimi did it. Mimi would tell me not to believe a single word that came out of my son's mouth because it was all lies.

For a while there, Mimi wanted to rent her farmhouse to us, and once we told her we wanted to find our own place, because she started becoming extremely controlling, she lied and told everyone that I chose my boyfriend over my son and cut all contact between my son and me for a week. I later found out she had him in the children's psych ward of East Alabama Medical Center, and wasn't going to tell me about it. How dare this bitch. Mimi said that the triangular manipulation my son did between her and her husband just about caused them to get a divorce. I later found out the drinking he was doing caused that. She had my son parroting her, saying that being in the psych ward was like a vacation, and he had a good time.

I was a concerned mother and did my research and got my son's medical records, and the doctor himself said that my son was perfectly normal. She tried really hard to get the doctor to believe her bull shit, so that she could draw a check off of my son. She had my son on medications, which my son told me made him feel really bad, so I took him off of the meds. This woman never cared about my son, and the justice center is trash.

Chapter 22

LIVING BUT NOT REALLY LIVING

——————

Once Trex started living with us, everything was perfect. I screwed up trying to be his friend before his mother, when really I didn't know how to be a mom myself. I had to teach myself everything, and my entire childhood was a complete joke; there wasn't anyone who consistently stayed in my life. So at first Trex got whatever he wanted; he would throw fits when he didn't, and I was the first one to call his Mimi, and she would get on the phone with him, and it was like a light switch my son would stop crying, and behave. I'm not sure what she said to him but it scared the shit out of him.

The marine was nice to my son at first, but then both the marine and I started learning that my son wasn't as innocent as he portrayed. The marine figured that out quicker than I did. I still sided with my son no matter what. So the marine and I were at it all the time over the way I was raising my son and how I was letting him do whatever he wanted to do. It got to the point where I was at home full time and the marinade was supporting us. In the beginning, he gave me access to his debit cards and let me pay the bills and buy dope. In fact, right when we first met, I made him go to my dope dealer's hotel room and buy my dope just to make sure he wasn't the police. The marine was bad with money; he always tried putting the bills last and always wanted to go out to eat when we had food in our refrigerator.

For a while, when things got normal and everyone got situated, I got comfortable and would leave my son with his best friend at the house with the marine alone. I acted like I had not a worry in the world. I would tell the marine I was going to go get dope and I wouldn't be back till the next day. I would get caught up with this other guy. I went dumpster diving with him, and we would get geeked up and lose track of time. I found some texts in the marine's phone with him asking his ex-wife for some nude pictures, and I just said screw this shit I'm gonna do whatever I want to do. Honestly, my son wasn't my first priority and I regret it today. I decided I was going to sleep with this guy that I would run off on my fun sprees with just to get back at the marine, and I wasn't even attracted to him. It was one of my worst mistakes in Alabama.

I eventually found out the Marine never cared; he was the type of guy that wasn't loyal, and would never be loyal. He stepped out on his first wife and then me, and then I knew for a fact stepped out a few times on his current girlfriend. He even tried contacting me after our relationship had ended. I turned around and screenshotted the text and sent them to his current girlfriend. Once a dog, always a dog. During this time, my son was pretty much doing whatever he wanted; it was all my fault.

I should have been a better mom, and the marine stopped paying for anything; he wouldn't help me pay for my son's sports, or field trips. I wasn't working, and the Marine still expected sex from me. I cut him off quickly, and when I did, he cut us off. The marine would sit in the living room when he wasn't at work and watch war movies, which scared my son, and his friends. I was also freaked out about it. My son would always tell me this guy was weird and I would never listen, because I was so preoccupied with where and when I was going to get dope. The marine loved it when I was high because he would have a chance to have sex with me. I grew to be disgusted with the sight of this guy. I was out running errands one day, and I came home and my son and his friend, Dylan, told me that the marine picked Trex up by the throat and held him over the front porch and was threatening to drop him.

I ran to tell my dumpster diving friend what was going on, and he snapped and got sick of the marine beating me, putting his hands on my child and the marine talking to me like he owned me. My friend literally ran up in my living room and beat the shit out of the marine. I remember trying to break it up and the three of us went flying through a two and half inch thick glass coffee table. The marine didn't even have the chance to blink. He was out on the floor in a fetal position, and my buddy was out the door. A part of me was so happy this happened, and the marine really deserved it.

This outbreak caused the marine to leave without any of his shit. He left without paying any of the bills and it was already the third, so it was just me and Trex. I tried to figure out what to do, so that we don't get kicked out, and I resorted to calling everyone in my family begging for 800.00 dollars while crying and screaming. Finally, spoke with my father and he agreed to give me the money but warned never to hear my voice again. My father didn't know what was going on, but he really didn't care either. So he sent me the money through western union and I paid our bills, and then found a job with Walmart two days later. God was working.

I had just got out of an abusive relationship with an ex-marine, someone with absolutely no personality, and a waste of three years. We won't talk about the him much because he doesn't deserve to take part in this journey you're learning about.

Chapter 23

WEIRDO

―――――

"Shit," the pigs in a blanket were scattered all over the kitchen floor. I had been running around the house all day trying to maintain my high, and figure up a way to throw a birthday party for a 12 year old boy, getting him gifts with food stamps, because I needed to learn how to prioritize, and say no to things, especially when your child didn't earn them. On any other day outside of special occasions, my son got whatever he wanted. Adding addiction to this story made our lives unmanageable. It's 2021 tweens are asking for $100.00 sneakers, and $400.00 game systems, and don't respect their parents, and act entitled to everything. It's my fault, and I own it. I played best friend, instead of mom in my son's life. That Disneyland phase ended quickly.

2021 was a bad year for us; my kid was brought up not appreciating things that a lot of people don't have such food on the table, a roof over your head, and the long hours parents put in to make all of this possible. My son was influenced by the other family—his on and off again family. They never respected me; therefore, my son didn't either, and adding addiction made it a lot worse. I thought I was doing enough for him, but the love and quality time I should have provided for my son was the one thing he needed the most, but love was one thing i couldn't even do for myself. I didn't know how to love. I could care less about myself; all I knew to care for was a high that consumed most of the best years of my life. The high protected me from reality, trauma. I tried covering up because I didn't understand it. Little did I know everything would surface and I would have to face everything once I decided to get on the right path. Keep reading; you have to go through the storm to get to the rainbow. I lived a life with a veil over my head. My life had been an act, a show, and as long as no one knew what really was going on, I thought we were going to be ok. Who wants to live, but not really live? It's a lonely life, and extremely selfish and confusing for everyone that loves you; you end up pushing everyone away. Now that I look back I robbed my son of a mother, something he truly deserved, and my daughter. They were victims of circumstances, so was Weirdo and myself.

I heard a knock on my door, and I answered. Then weirdo, his wife, and her current boyfriend walked in. This happened during my son's birthday. I was always one to judge a book by its cover, and would always call a dope head out, and gossip with coworkers, as they would laugh, so would I. The first thing that crossed my mind was redneck trailer park trash, "God forgive me." My son and his friends got through eating and started with the Xbox. So I thought my duties were done. My next duty was to escape and figure out a way to get dope. Truly, the only thing

I thought about was dope. I tried breaking away, but Weirdo's wife wouldn't shut the hell up. I finally left the party to go and get a sack, and when I returned weirdo was outside playing football. I'll never forget that picture. There was warmth about this picture. I now understand; back then I felt it was normal I was a very selfish addict.

Accountability is something I still struggle with. I regret things that I know now I don't have the power to change. You can't go back in time, but you sure as hell can move forward and try your hardest to become the best version of yourself, in hopes your loved ones will later understand. It wasn't too long before Weirdo and I realized we were extremely alike. November 12, 2023 will make us a couple for four years. I managed to maintain a relationship with a man that I didn't deserve; neither of us was at our best potential. He absolutely worshipped the ground that I walk on, and back then I couldn't understand why.

Crystal Meth turned us into monsters; anything and everything I would screw up I would put all the blame on Weirdo. He was my scapegoat or at least that's what I thought. I would be late for work, and for a couple of our jobs we had, we worked together. I would tell our bosses that Weirdo wouldn't get out of bed, or he lost the keys and we couldn't find them. Truth was all my insecurities were heightened on meth, to where I would stand in the mirror ridiculing everything about myself. I had a routine that I had to follow or else I couldn't start my day. My showers consisted of washing my feet with foot scrub, shaving my legs even when there wasn't hair to shave, tipping my belly button out, and my ears, flat ironing my hair till I completely destroyed it, and tweaking my eyebrows, literally off. I mean I had no eyebrows. I would draw them on, which took an hour because I had to have everything perfect, but on dope nothing is ever perfect. I looked like a drag queen, and through this all Weirdo still loved me. Yet I cared less; dope was overpowering, and when I found out Weirdo did dope too, I ran with it. I pawned my son off on him. I pawned all my responsibilities on Weirdo. When I met Weirdo, I called him Peter Pan because there was innocence about him, He would give anyone the shoes off his feet. I mean anyone. When Weirdo got high, he would do whatever I asked him to do. He built me a pallet fence around our entire mobile home, replaced a French drain, leveled my backyard so that I could have a garden, built an awesome shed for us out of pallets, put a bathtub in when all I had was a shower, and all I did was bitch at him for his shortcomings. I'm in disgust now that I look back and see how awful and ungrateful I was. Weirdo still believed God sent him to me, and he still stuck it out. My son loved Weirdo in the beginning but after some time weirdo and I were doing just enough for my son but not enough. We were in a world that wasn't reality. I know my son knew something was different about us. Weirdo was absent minded when it came to leaving paraphernalia lying around. I thought I hid my paraphernalia and always covered my tracks. Or at least that's what I thought. When you're doing drugs as much as we were, you forget about the things that actually matter. You open doors to negativity and evil things. I would call it Pandora's box..

My son went from being an active happy kid to a depressed, unmotivated, lazy, and disrespectful child, in what it seemed like overnight. He started gaining a ton of weight, and never wanted to leave his room. He was always glued to his Xbox. Now that I look back I know it was a result of me isolating myself in my room while I got high. I would stay in my room pretending I was taking a nap and yell for Weirdo to make sure he fed my son breakfast, lunch, and dinner. I was pitiful. I was bound by the devil. As I type this, I remember my actions. It brings tears to my eyes. I wished I knew how to love then. Love wasn't in my vocabulary; it just wouldn't click to me. I couldn't grasp the concept of love.

Chapter 24

DEJAVU

Narrators insert:

I'm grateful for the sober feelings of joy, pain, grief. I'm able to endure, and understand now what I didn't understand before. I had so much to do, but not enough time. Rummaging through my clothes, I finally found something to wear after changing my outfit four or five times, "Good grief." If I could just focus on one thing at a time, I might have finished something in a timely manner." It's impossible to focus or even be productive in society when you're under any mind altering substances.

"Mom! Mom! Mom!" My son cried while walking out of the front door, "will you bring home some burger king?"

"Sure kid. Do you think you can have your room cleaned up?" I respond sarcastically to my son. It was too early in the morning to be serious. We laughed. "I love you son," I said affectionately.

"I love you too mom," he replied.

Around 6 pm, I pulled up into our driveway. "Guys come help me get these groceries in," I shout out. "Come on guys," I said as I walked in with four grocery bags hanging off each arm. I saw Weirdo Sitting on the couch. He was looking like he had just seen a ghost. I knew something was wrong as I walked in my son's room and noticed that the TV, game system, computer, and the clothes from his closet I just got him with my tax return were all gone—except for the dirty dishes he said he would get up. My home no longer felt like a home, or the facade I was trying to portray. Deja vu reality started to sink in a little too late. It's never on time; when your priorities are not right and dope is your life. This wouldn't be the first time I lost my son. God gave me five years to get things right, and I ignored Him. I didn't care honestly. I really didn't know how to care. There was that knot that I was so familiar with in the back of my throat but I couldn't explain it. I wanted to cry, but I did this, not for only me, but my son and Weirdo had to suffer.

Narrators insert:

After my son was taken from our home, this is what I did: I went to retrieve my child and bring him home. I did whatever any other mother would have done.

Chapter 25

NOTASULGA AL. POLICE

"Mame, there's not much we can do, your son is in a different jurisdiction, but you are more than welcome to file a police report," a police officer said to me. It was all happening before my eyes again. I lost all power, but I was still determined to retrieve my son from the on and off again family. I pulled up at the driveway, and approached the man of the house respectfully. "What's going on? Where's my son?" I asked nervously. "I'm here to pick my son up," I added. Mimi and her daughter were walking out. Her daughter had this grin on her face. From what I remember it was empathetic, and rude, but her daughter always acted like her shit doesn't stink. I hate to break it to her, but she's got a long road to travel, and in the real world, it doesn't pay to be ugly to people. "You need to get back into your truck and get the hell off of my property. Mimi said hatefully, "Get off my property before I get you off my property." The man of the house yelled. Mimi said, "Narcy, you might want to listen, or else." I refused to get off their property. I was doing what any other parent would do, and tried retrieving my son.

I had physical/primary custody. There were no police reports, claiming abuse or neglect, and there were no hospital records. Legally, what right did they have removing my son from my home, as well as trying to remove him from school? If it were such a bad home, why didn't someone call the police? Why wouldn't anyone let me see my son? How was I supposed to know he was ok? Was he even at their house? My mind went running in a million different directions.

The man of the house took a chain and wrapped it around the back of my bumper and dragged me out into the middle of the road damaging my bumper. If my son was inside, what type of role models were these people? Their entire family remained in the driveway laughing at me, and I still didn't see my son. "I'm not leaving without my son." I yelled, and they continued mocking me.

The next day, I returned with a copy of the joint custody agreement that I had signed years ago. I was determined to retrieve my son. I went and sat at the Notasulga Police Department, and literally waited three hours for the sheriff to show up. I didn't want to go to the on and off again families' house and another episode as the last occurred. I needed police witnesses. I explained to the sheriff what was going on, and they asked me what the address was and I couldn't remember. I had only been to their new home in Notasulga two times before, and my sense of direction was awful. The sheriff told me to follow him because he knew the address, and he knew exactly who I was talking about. I was sober. Mimi's husband was an ex-police officer. This sheriff was extremely disrespectful. I followed him and headed to their home. I thought I was going to pick my son up. The officer began speeding driving above 60 miles per hour, and he made it impossible for me to keep up. I remember getting so frustrated, and pulling into a random driveway, and about 15 minutes later, a different officer pulled up behind me, and I ended up following him to the house. The deputy was already at their home laughing it up with the on and off again family. This was day two and I still did not see my son. Mimi said he was off with some friends, I was frustrated and I knew something wasn't right.

I got out of my truck with the paperwork as both officers were walking toward me. I showed the officer my custody agreement. It clearly stated that Mimi was to get my approval before picking my son up. It was a Sunday evening. She had had my son for three days. Even in the documents, she awarded one weekend out of the month, with my approval, to pick him up on Friday and bring him back on Sunday. The officer ignored everything, and said "Well, this is her time to get your son."

It was Sunday and the time to return my son to me had passed. If we were really going by the custody agreement, then they had breached its terms. The police didn't give a fuck. They claimed they didn't want to be involved in the middle of civil matters. If the shoe were on the other foot, and the cops were not crooked, my son would have been returned to me, and Mimi and her husband should have been incarcerated. It was like pulling teeth to get the on and off again family to spend time with my son when my son lived with me. It broke my heart every time they canceled on my son. So the bull shit that's going on here is true caca. What's right is right, and what's wrong is wrong. The cops were biased and crooked as fuck. The on and off again family dangled my son over my head the five years he lived with me, making it impossible to have the relationship my son and I deserved.

I own the fact that I was using but no one else was aware; it doesn't make it right. I know I later found out both Notasulga officers were friends with the on and off again family on Facebook. What made this sad was that I was naive all along. I thought the police were going to do the right thing because they are supposed to protect everyone. Instead they illegally failed to do their duties as a police department, and bullied me, making me a mockery. Not once did anyone care about my son's best interest because if they did none of this would have happened. If I was sober I could have kept this from happening. My son wouldn't be growing up in a home where people were taught to judge others, and to look down on them, or taught not to appreciate your God given name. Classmates make fun of it, and not to appreciate your background, and culture, to the point that you want to change your last name. The on and off again family laughed and made fun of my son's last name. He's being taught that it's ok to disrespect your parents, and taught not to appreciate shit. I tried instilling love in my son. I remember buying him a notebook and telling him to write in it every time he felt bullied or needed to tell me something while he was in school, and I would look at it when he came home.

During all of this bull shit, I was going through the few things that were left behind the day he left and I found my son's notebook. My son was being bullied, not just by his classmates but by his science teacher as well. I was teaching my son how to stand up for himself and apparently he did, but the teacher made him feel worthless. My son was singing in this class, and the teacher blatantly said, "If that's the best voice you have, it's awful," and made fun of him. This is what our teachers are teaching our kids—how to bully. Apparently this middle/high school had had this issue for generations. Finally, a parent had the nerve to speak up, but this world lives as if they weren't given a mind of their own, and they have to be followers and not leaders—they were just a bunch of cowards, in my opinion.

Narrators Insert:

I dream that both my kids grow up to treat everyone equally, and to help heal this world.

Chapter 26

EMERGENCY COURT HEARING

―――――

"Ms. Elmogahzy, you look taller since the last time you were in my courtroom," the judge said.

"Yes sir. It's been awhile," I replied. My head drooped down and I tried to fight the tears. I was ashamed. I saw my son sitting next to his on and off again family, and not once did he look my way. Mimi's (she's not related to us at all. I'll explain more as we go) attorney went to talk about Weirdo. Weirdo wasn't even in the courtroom to defend himself. Mimi's attorney talked about Weirdo, how my son had walked in and saw a bag on my bed with Weirdo, filled with a substance.. Then went on to ask if there was in fact alcohol in my home, and I truthfully said there was a bottle of wine in the house for the past six months. Weirdo brought it home from a home we cleaned. It had been there ever since. We weren't planning on drinking it, so it sat there collecting dust. Honestly, we completely forgot about it. Weirdo respected the fact that I will always be a recovering alcoholic and he chose not to drink around me or my son. We had Weirdo's brother over one New Year and Weirdo drank two beers with his brother as we shot fireworks which was the most alcohol Weirdo has drank out of the three years we had been together. I've had troubles with alcohol abuse and a result from it led to me losing custody of my son on two different occasions in the past.

The attorney went on to say, "Is it true that Weirdo tore your son's door down, and cut the WIFI off so that your son couldn't call his Mimi?" Truth be told, I was geeked up in my room. At that time I was sorry as hell and pawned all my responsibilities on Weirdo. As a mother, I should have got off my ass, put the glass pipe down, and get my son out of bed myself. Instead I sent Weirdo. By this time my son was getting out of control. He was retaliating against us because I wasn't doing my duties as his mother. "I'm not going to school. You can't fucking make me. You're a fat bitch." "Not again kid." I was shouting from my room. Weirdo was in the bedroom with me, but after hearing my son, he wasn't there for long. Weirdo flung our bedroom door open, and stormed down the hallway to my son's room. "You don't yell at your mom like that. Get your ass out of bed and get ready for school," he said. I've never seen Weirdo that upset. I think he just got tired, and all of the responsibilities I put on him, with no appreciation, caught up with him, and he had enough.

Weirdo got a drill and unhinged the door. He disconnected the Wi-Fi so my kid couldn't play his Xbox and he might get up and get ready for school, and the door was removed because you don't disrespect your adults and slam the door in their faces. My son always threatened to tell Mimi whenever he didn't get his way around the house. It really affected my role as his mother when she constantly belittled me and disrespected me in before my son. How would he ever respect me when the people who cared for my son want my son to be with me for reasons, more selfish. With God, justice will surface, and we will all have to pay our dues for dancing with the devil. I will get my son back. It's just a matter of time, and patience.

Narrator insert:

God makes your life unmanageable, and takes everything and anyone you love away, until you tighten up. I take complete accountability for everything that I have done to get me in situations like these. You have to change; you have to want better for yourself. Your kids are counting on you. Don't let anyone tell you your children do not love you. That would be a lie.

Chapter 27

BATE

In the first two months, I called the other family every day begging to speak with my son. I just needed to hear his voice, to know he was ok. She would answer each day and tell me my son didn't want to speak to me and she would blow me off. She never asked me to go and take a drug test; she literally just cut me off of all contact. Then finally after two months, Mimi tricked me into believing she wanted to help restore our relationship, and she would bring my son over to our house for us to sit down and talk. One thing I still don't understand is the man of the house in the on and off again family. He was a recovering alcoholic, and no one could tell me that he and his wife didn't get into arguments around their children. No one took their kids away when things got bad. I know this and any other recovering alcoholic knows that it's a hell of a roller coaster to ride. Mimi never turned her kids against her husband, so why were they any different from Weirdo, me and Trex?. My son and Mimi pulled up at my driveway, and my son walked in the house first. She was behind him, forcing her way in as well. She was being kind, and that was short-lived. Once she let herself in my home, she said to my son, "Aren't you going to ask your mother for your things?" My son shrugged his shoulders. I told them his things will remain with me until he returned home. Mimi got angry and told me my son hated my attitude. Then she spat in my face. Then she went to say to my son and said to him, "Aren't you going to ask your mom for your dog and your cat?"

The off and on again family already got my son. I thought about how he would get the two things my son ignored while living with me. At first, I didn't care for animals but watching my son ignore them, I took over the role of caring for them. They followed me around everywhere. My son didn't respond to her. I looked at her and told her she had already taken my son, and it would be unfair to strip me of my animals. They were part of our family. I was trying to hold it together but this woman had run me through the dirt year after year. You will learn as you continue reading how Mimi showed her true color. Mimi pulled the court documents out, a new court order, which I never received a copy. It clearly stated that I was to give both my cat and dog to them. My son was silent the entire time. Was this woman typing and printing out her own court documents? If this arrangement was supposed to be in my son's best interest, what had the family court system become? How was this demonstrating a good role model for my son?

It showed him how to continue disrespecting me more. My son finally spoke, and he said he wanted to see his father. I told my son it was because of me that was possible, because Mimi would have left my son's father out of everything if she could, as she had done many times before. She told the court she didn't know where my son's father was.

The on and off again family didn't care about the one visit I was court ordered to have. I continued calling them every day and begging to speak and visit with my son, and finally Mimi let me speak with my son. His responses were one word responses each time I asked him a question. I asked him about our cat and dog.

You could tell the phone was on speaker and Mimi said quickly, "Your dog is dead. I could hear my son crying, and all I could say was, "Ason, it's not your fault. I'm not mad at you. There is nothing you could ever do to make me upset with you."

He said, "Mom I'm sorry." I told him again none of this was his fault. I told him that I loved him, and he muttered through his tears, "I love you too mom." All of this was a result of him not getting his way when I didn't buy him an iPhone 11 and him calling Mimi and out of anger telling her everything that was going on in our home. I knew right then and there that he truly wanted to come home. I felt it in his voice, but he couldn't say anything because he knew that what Mimi said was accepted, that's where he had to lay his head. Moreover, these people provided for his needs. Why was it the only time I was allowed to speak to my son? It's sad. It's as if Mimi wanted any memory that my son and I had ever had together to be sad, bad, or mad. I. I've had it. I have taken accountability for all my fuck ups; now it's Mimi's turn. My son would need lots of therapy. Why won't she do the right thing: give my son and myself the opportunity to have a loving and nurturing, healthy relationship before it's too late. This woman is beyond cruel.

My son's father suffered from alcoholism, just like Mimi's husband did, sober or not. We are all recovering addicts/alcoholics, and no one is better than anyone. Mimi alienated my son's father and that entire side of the family, as well as myself. She held my son over all of our heads. We all make mistakes. It takes some of us longer than others to realize them. Thank God for sobriety. This would be the last time I saw my son. April of 2021.

Narrators insert:

My son's father is now dead. My son could have spent more time with his father, and should be a part of his father's family. They are awesome people. What part of this does Mimi see healthy for my child? There were numerous occasions my son's father and I were sober and doing really well. Mimi still chose to alienate my son from us. What was or is she hiding?

Everything that was said in the courtroom that day was twisted beyond measure. The fucked up thing about it all was everything was blamed on Weirdo and I allowed it. I'm not sure if my son's Mimi instilled what was said in the courtroom in my son, and my son was just parroting her or my son was just trying to protect me. I honestly doubt I'll ever know the truth. There isn't an excuse for the system to ruin a good man's name in a courtroom, when that man isn't even present to defend himself. There was never an investigation, and no charges were ever filed, so what part of any of this is legal? I rose, and requested for the judge to take my son to his quarters and ask him there, so there wouldn't be pressure and he could make a decision, and not feel bad about it. The judge returned to the court room without my son.

I specifically told the judge that wherever my son chose to live as long as he was happy I was happy. The judge said he chose his on and off again family. I was shocked, and in disbelief because not even two weeks prior I made my child spend the entire spring break with his on and off again family because I believed it to be better for him than to be at home isolated in his room and glued to the Xbox. Nearly two days later, Mimi called me and said, "He's already ready to come home. What should I do"?

It doesn't help that the on and off again family was well plugged in. Their kids grew up in the same schools as the judges, played in some of the same sports, and went to some of the same churches. The judge and Mimi were both Alumni's and Mimi's husband was an ex-cop. The whole situation was biased, and none of the hearing was done by the book. The only thing that the court documents stated was that my son and the other family desired for my son to live with them, and that I agreed. What criminal charges were made, and what proof of neglect was proven? Before a child is removed from a home, there has to be an investigation. The removal of my son was illegal, and literally everything was falsified. I tell this story with a sober mind. Mimi's attorney wrote it up to her liking, and everyone involved signed off on it.

I messed up five years ago. Now the on and off again family literally threw my son back at me after calling my sister and telling her they couldn't care for him anymore. I was in disbelief, and beyond thrilled. I was getting my son back. I signed in relief to share joint legal custody with this family with myself having physical custody when I should have got my son and ran, but God knew I wasn't good at this time. Even though they may not have known what I was doing, God did.

Narrator Insert:

I resented this family for a long time, but now I'm thankful to God they exist in a matter. Considering I have been given many opportunities to get my act together, yet I didn't make the right decisions. I selfishly put my son in this situation. Everything happens for a reason. I know but, as I mentioned earlier, accountability can be a hard pill to swallow. I can genuinely say that I am thankful for sobriety today, because as I sit here in this library I am clear headed and aware of my thoughts and actions and wouldn't fall back into the fantasy world that active addiction bounded me before. I am able to slip right back into reality, a place I find extremely hard mentally and emotionally hard to face. I'm finally free and greatness doesn't come easily. I am prepared for whatever obstacles I may encounterthat may come my way in the future. I'm prepared and protected by my God. He continues providing for both Weirdo and me, and you will understand more as you read. I know this was God protecting my child. Things should have been handled a lot differently.

The judge and no one else knew about my drug use, so I stood up and told the judge that if in fact my son desired to live with the on and off again family, and that was the family's desires as well, I wouldn't pay child support. The judge asked the family if they were able to support my son, and they answered, "Yes, more than able." So the judge waived my child support. He granted me at least one visit a month with my son under the on and off again family's discretion and for Weirdo not to have any contact with my son. I will admit Weirdo and I would fight like cats and dogs.

Drugs could do that to you, and my son probably just got sick of it. Who could blame him? Or did he really tell the judge he wanted to live with the other family or not. This will never be known. I asked the judge during court that if I took a drug test, and passed it, could my son come home with me, and the judge said not necessarily. What I didn't understand was what right they had for taking my child. My son got mad over an iPhone 11 that I couldn't afford. That's not a good enough reason to remove a child from their home. I offered to take a drug test. I knew I would fail, but the judge didn't. Court ended and as everyone left the courtroom, and the judge and I were the last ones remaining, he said, "Ms. Elmogahzy, I'm going to need you to go and take a hair follicle test and pay $180.00 and bring it to me in three days, or have it faxed here. I had spent all my money that I received from taxes on my drugs, and had no money. The judge requested it off the books, just like my son was removed unlawfully. I didn't follow through. I contacted the judge a week later and told him it wasn't documented and I didn't have the money to pay for it. The next day, I received a retyped court order ordering me to take a hair follicle test from the crooked judge. He made sure it was documented. Instead of the on and off again family encouraging the reunification between my son and myself, they made a mockery and a joke of me to him, so I decided I had had enough. I had to become strong, strong enough to get what I wanted—to protect my kids, and to be confident enough to go mock on these doors, request for my kids to come outside, and get in my car. I was almost there. I was able to pick my kids up, and finally bring them home.

Narrators insert:

God was telling me it was time for me to step it up, and heal, so that one day, I am strong enough to be the mother both of my kids needed. So I sucked it up, and it hurt. Don't get me wrong. I realized I had to fix myself before I could be good for anyone. I realized God stuck it out with me through the good and the bad, and He is going the rest of the way with me. I just have to be patient, and start living right. I realized I didn't have a chance at building a good relationship with my son, until I got right, with God and myself.

Chapter 28

BREAKING POINT

———

There were many events that led to Weirdo and I leaving Alabama, we were living in Beauregard AL. In a trailer park on a dirt road, everyone in that trailer park was related, set in their ways, on dope, dealing dope, trying to set people up, gang stalking, the people in this trailer park were low vibration, always gossiping, snooping around. They would be kind to your face, but ugh… I wasn't going to put this in my book, but I'm speaking my truth. I am the type of person who loves to see people doing great in their lives. It makes me happy, but this trailer park made our lives hell. These people hated to see us doing well.

It all began before I met Weirdo, I was dating a marine. My dope dealer lived in the first trailer on our dirt road, everytime i had problems with the marine I would run over there and tell this old, hateful, man all of my business. In the beginning I was naive and thought my dope dealer was my friend. Little did I know he would use all of this against me for years to come. This dope dealer would crum me, and rip me off everytime i bought dope from him, because he knew he could get away with it. He tried for the longest time to have sex with me but i wouldn't ever give in, i found out later on he told everyone that we slept together. I wouldn't dare. Gross.

There was a guy we will call him Joe, him, his wife, and daughter lived a couple trailers up from us. He was considered the maintenance man for my landlord, and was always helping everyone out, at times i would get him to get me dope when i couldn't get dope from the dope man, because for some reason or another i was being cut off because i would call my dope man out, and he would explode in rage, call me a whore, and every disgusting name in the book. In all actuality he was worse than scum. I knew Joe wasn't someone to be trusted, he was always out all hours of the night creeping around. No one on dope should be trusted, it took a lot of trials for me to finally wake up to reality. Joe's daughter had a huge crush on my son. I believe this neighborhood of low vibrational people had everything to do with my son hating his life. I believe my son knew things that were going on around in our neighborhood, that I was unaware of because I would always be at work after the marine left us, and my son would be at home alone.

There were a handful of people I let my son hangout with, My dope dealer had a nephew that lived up the street. I would take my son to's house so that they could play every now and again, and then there's this family right behind our trailer park that I would let my son go over and play with their boys almost everyday. This family asked me one day if my son could bring his xbox over; they already had one, but i agreed naive as i was then. All of my credentials were used to open a microsoft xbox account so that my son can play his games, later that evening

when my son returned with his xbox, I lost access to two of my gmail accounts, and the passwords were changed, so that i couldn't get back into my accounts. I tried absolutely everything to regain access. The more my son spent time with this family, his attitude changed, not for the good, but extremely disrespectful. My son and these two boys ended up going to my sons mimi's house one weekend and they were all suppose to stay the entire weekend, riding four wheelers, but they didn't even make it one day, my sons Mimi calls me and tells me all the boys are wanting to come back to my house. So they return. I put an end to my son spending time with this family, because one day I was outside doing yard work, and my son was running down the dirt road bawling, just crying hysterically from their home, and I asked him what happened and he refused to tell me. I can recall en extremely awkward moment while i was at the Walmart working, these boys parents came to the exact aisle i was stocking items on and literally lingered on that aisle for 40 minutes without saying a word to me just both of them on their cell phones doing God knows what, and what made it awkward was i was stocking items on an african american hair aisle this couple is caucasian. To me they were either trying to scare me, or they were posting up to make sure I was where I was, because something was going on at my home that I wasn't aware of, or that's what they wanted me to think. I sent a text to this couple the next day, and instantly I was gaslighted and told I was crazy, but literally for 40 minutes they were on their phones on this aisle that I was stocking on. Why not any other aisle, it would be different if it were the caucasian hair product aisle. When Weirdo and I started dating things started to get extremely strange, Everytime Weirdo and i would go to fighting he would run across the street and tell the neighbors what was going on, he would tell Joe the maintenance guy and he would tell everyone in the neighborhood, and these people would feed off of the drama, and at the time during active addiction you tend to be a follower and definitely not a leader, he would talk down on me to everyone around out of anger, he would stay the night with the neighbors across the street every so often.

Joe rubbed me the wrong way one afternoon when i was walking our dog, and i stopped to talk to him, and he asked me where my son was, and i told him he was playing his xbox, and Joe goes on to say your son is a really behaved boy, and to me, i thought how would you know how behaved my son was. Joe was acting like he knew my son, but my son and him to my knowledge never held a conversation. It made me wonder what was going on in my trailer park when I was at work. Everyone in the trailer park knew what time I worked, and what time I got off work, a female across the street and her brother both worked at the same Walmart as me. There were many times different people in my trailer park literally followed me to, from work, and many different places I would go. I used to think it was paranoia because of the drugs, but it got to the point that I would purposely pull into a dead end road park, and this white vehicle would pull in right after me, and it was this same white vehicle each time. This left me in fear, to go anywhere, or do anything. One morning my landlord called me and told me the night before there was a white truck parked in a vacant lot two trailers down from mine, she said two men got out, went around to my back door and were trying to get in, she said she wasn't sure if they got in or not. At the time I was at work and Weirdo and my son were at the house. I questioned Weirdo and my son, as to why they didn't tell me about it and my son got extremely defensive and said for me not to yell at Weirdo. My question is, how did my landlord know that there were two men at my back door, trying to pry into my home, but neither my son or Weirdo knew??? Then another family who lived in twin pines trailer park i would have to drive my son a little ways so that he would be able to hang out with them. That friendship ended quickly at Twin Pines, he said the boys always were covered in poop, and he wasn't ever allowed to play the game system with them. Plus I allowed my son to go to the skate center with his family, and he was supposed to be back by 8pm that evening. These people took him to Columbus Ga. without letting me know, as I'm at home freaking out, and he's not returned until 3 or 4 am. I was worried sick, and these people didn't care.

One event that scared the living shit out of me, was when i told my son he could go to his friend Martin's house after school, one afternoon, but he wasn't to leave or go anywhere with anyone, until i picked him up. My son knows better than to do such a thing. I even spoke to Martin's mom and we agreed on this. I leave work and go to pick my son up, and my son isn't where he was supposed to be. My son ended up leaving Martin's house with my dope dealers nephew and my dope dealers lady best friend. Weirdo and i looked for my son went to the couple of peoples homes he could have gone to, with no information, until this kid that was playing outside in Martin's neighborhood, told us that my son left with Dope dealers nephew, and lady friend to go get ice cream, no one asked my permission, i didn't have this woman's phone number, and to me this was downright a crime. I went home, and waited patiently. What made the situation way worse is my dope man and Joe knew exactly where my son was and watched me freaking out, and didn't say a word. This woman had my son for 4 hours, and i had no idea what ice cream shop they were at, and finally we got this woman's number from the dope man, and i call her, and she says, "you fucking bitch, ill bring your God damn son home when i feel like it", she said, "this is what you get for messaging my husband and asking him for money, you fucking whore", i mean her words were so ugly. I couldn't believe this was happening. Her husband messaged me telling me how he was single, which I could care less about. At the time I was an active user and I asked to borrow some money and this was a month prior. I completely forgot about this. I never even met with the guy. My son returns home and he is so disrespectful to me, and I mean my son said some of the most hateful things to me. He went into his room and didn't say anything about it. I'm disappointed in myself because if i was sober, i could have protected my son instead of fearing everything. I miss my son. More than words can ever express..

There were a few times I found panties that weren't mine, and mascara that wasn't mine in my home, things would go missing. I would question Weirdo about the panties, and he would say his wife probably came into our home and put them there to start shit, or someone was doing things for us to argue. A part of me truly believes this. It got so strange we ended up getting cameras inside and outside of our home. We lived in fear, and all along it was the people in our trailer park doing these things. We literally ran out of Alabama. God protected us the entire time, i'll tell y'all this because i know i would have been swallowed alive, if i stayed any longer. I want you guys that have been through anything like this to know, you are not crazy, it happens to the best of us. You can not let the evil in the world win. You have to gain the courage to get out, and become the best version of yourself.

Narrators insert:

Being sober, has made me wonder if back in 2017 when My sons other family, basically threw my son at me, when i was living in the motel, drinking, drugging, prostituting, and them not knowing this quote on quote boyfriend (marine) that i met on an online dating site, it's made me wonder if "the other family", already knew the, "Marine"?. Why else if you cared so much about my son would you give him to me so freely??.. Life goes on, we heal, and we understand that everything that has happened in our lives was necessary for us to become who God put us on this planet to be.

Chapter 29

LIFE OR DEATH

▬▬▬▬

Weirdo had this unconditional love for me. He still has it and I'm lucky to have this man. I was going to show him the world. This man hasn't seen any other state but Alabama, and Chicago for a concert he went to. In my heart, his life was worth saving. I love him. I honestly believe God really did send him to me to protect me; we protect each other, so he and I decided to go on a journey of a lifetime.

Weirdo and I got in my Chevrolet Tahoe and at first we were just going to drive to Atlanta Ga. and door dash to make a bunch of money and then return, and buy a bunch of dope and go on a binge for a week. However, on our way, we started meeting some really cool people. They were good people and we started realizing there was more in this world than getting high. We weren't ready to give up; we wanted to see the world. We were sick and tired of being sick and tired. Our goal ended up changing and we were going to Door dash around the United States, and get sober together. I wanted to find my biological mother. She had dementia and I wanted to catch her before it got worse and she couldn't remember, and it would be full blown altzhimers. I needed to tell her that I forgave her, no matter what, and that I loved her. All of this became a healing process for us. We weren't aware of the magic that was divinely set in our paths. God had a plan and we were following it. Little did we know this was going to be a divine intervention that our spirits yearned for.

We left Alabama behind. We left a flat screen tv, another vehicle, brand new bottles of perfume, a shed full of tools, and a home, our home, and a brand new sewing machine. I really wanted to learn how to sew at least 30 pairs of tennis shoes. In my garden, I had two peach trees, two blueberry bushes, and a lot of beautiful plants. We knew if we stayed in Alabama, we would die, or end up incarcerated. It started out that we would door dash in Atlanta, then return home, because you made more money in Atlanta than we ever made in Alabama, and we wanted to get sober. We made a vow to never return to Alabama unless it was just to visit; we met new people, prettier surroundings, more opportunities and we saw that there was more to life in Atlanta—just imagine what else we would venture into, there was still the entire USA to explore.

We got on the road and made it to Georgia. Florida swam in the Gulf of Mexico. I no longer fear the ocean I used to not get in. I would fear sharks, but in this ocean you could see your feet. Louisiana, we made it to New Orleans. We didn't like it too much. Weirdo almost got shot just for walking up to a dude's car. When I was growing up in New Orleans as a child, it was a lot nicer—after hurricane Katrina it went to shit. While in Florida, we made it a point to go to the genealogy library and research my mother's side of the family, and we found out that my grandmother was in a nursing home, somewhere in Pensacola, which we went by five or six. No one could tell us because it was confidential, whether or not she was there. I posted all over social media names of people I was related to in hopes that someone would read my post and inbox me, but I had no luck, so we decided to get in our truck and continue with our journey.

Chapter 30

ATLANTA GA. TEMPTATION

So back in Atlanta Georgia, I'm going to go back just about in the beginning. Weirdo and I made it from Alabama to Atlanta Georgia, and there were some things I skipped over. Weirdo and I met this Hispanic guy whose name was Juan. He was a painter and had his own business. He hired Weirdo and me. We were excited to get hired to go and do this one job with him. We were helping him paint a house in a nice neighborhood, and Juan told me I would be working with him and Weirdo would be working on the other side of the house painting. So within the first two hours, Juan told me he used crystal meth, and I walked around front and told Robert we had to go because Juan used meth. I was new to sobriety and didn't want to risk it. Robert said, "Come on Narcy, let's finish this job then we will get this money and get back on the road. During this time, I thought that getting high one last time it won't hurt anything. So I told Weirdo I wanted to get high, and he said if I got high he would get high too. So Juan showed me the dope, and I starting getting excited. Juan snorted it, and I smoke it, so Juan didn't have the right paraphernalia I needed. So I told Juan and Weirdo that I was going to the gas station to buy a glass bowl so that I could smoke. In Alabama, we call it a chalet. I told them I would be right back.

In Alabama, Indian gas stations sold glass bowls for five or six dollars. The first gas station I went to the guy smirked and looked at me from behind the counter and said, "We don't sell that type of thing here." The second gas station told me the same thing but the guy was loud about it. I felt embarrassed and left. I wouldn't go back to Weirdo and Juan. I stayed out riding around for hours because I knew if I went back, I would get high. So my emotions were like a roller coaster. I was scared I didn't know anything about Atlanta but at the same time, I wanted to be clean. So in the midst of me driving around like a chicken with no head, I decided it was time to call the off and on again family (MIMI).

Narrators Insert:

I have learned quickly that I can't trust anyone, especially from Alabama, and especially my own blood. It's sad, but that's why God has given me another chance at life here in Austin Texas. I had to learn the hard way, to be choosy with who I allowed in my life. Life is too short.

My brother told them what was really going on. He told them why I wasn't the best mom that I could have been, and added that I left Weirdo with Juan and wasn't going back to get him because I wanted to get sober.

I honestly believed Weirdo had gotten high with Juan. He didn't look his normal self when I saw him earlier. Now that I'm thinking about it, both of us were coming off drugs. We were in the beginning phase, and neither of us looked normal. I was a wreck in the beginning of this journey. God bless. I begged Mimi to go and pick my two dogs up because I wouldn't be coming back. When I got healed, then I thought I could call my brother because I wanted to overcome my addictions. My brother was trying his hardest to find a way to pull my inheritance, and I had just made it easier. He had been asking around and no one in Alabama told him any of my businesses, so when I called him, all I said was, "Hey, I figured it out, things are going to start getting better for me." Then I told my brother I loved him, and hung up the phone. At this time, I felt alone, and thought I could trust Mimi, and Elmo and they would be happy. All I really wanted from my brother was to hear him say, "I love you too Narcy," when I told him I loved him. All I wanted him to say is I love you too. Now I accept the fact that my brother isn't who I wished him to be as a brother. I put him on this pedestal for so long and the clearer I get, the more I realize I made up this fantasy family to everyone, including myself, because in actuality, I didn't want anyone to know I had a crappy family. I wanted to be like everyone else. Well, that was what I thought every family was. I wanted people to think I had a family that had my back, and actually loved me. I wanted people to think in my times of being alone, I was spoken for, that I had a family, and no one could hurt me. I was a scared person. I had been hurt by many people without regard to my well-being for my entire life. I thank God for holding on to me.

Narrators insert:

I made a big mistake thinking my Brother or Mimi ever cared about my well-being. It was time to level up, and evolve into what God put me on this earth for. I needed to find my purpose. I had to get clean to face reality, and to understand and be honest with myself and accept things for what they really are.

Those few childhood memories are what stuck in my heart this entire time, and I managed to block out everything else. I gave credit, and spoke highly of my brothers and sisters to people because from what I saw on social media, they were doing well. I called them, at times just to see how they were doing, and I'll admit there were times during active addiction when I fell behind on bills, and I called them to ask for money, but I had no help from my brothers and sisters. My father helped me a total of four times since I was 16 years old, and that's the truth. Therefore, when my family says that I only called them when I needed money, it wasn't true. My conversations with my siblings became little to none.

I want those of you that have done what I've done, and made a fantasy image that you wanted people to think was real, to understand that you are beautiful, and you don't need anyone but yourself. At the end of the day, I guarantee your so-called family is going to need you before you will ever need them. Don't open your door for them. Promise me that you will close that door, and keep it shut, until you know they have been through what you have been through and become decent human beings. Otherwise don't waste another second on people who wouldn't do the same for you. Promise me this. I will tell you guys one thing my brother told me, and he was right. He said make your own friends and family, because the world is shit, and that will be the only advice that iI take from him ever in my life. I stand my ground, without ever again sugar coating shit. Don't give credit to those who don't deserve it. Remember they don't deserve it. Everyone, I pray that you become a leader and not a follower. I am taking action to change my paradigm.

It wasn't until my brother saw my posts for my documentary that he learned the truth. Then he literally lied to everyone, and made them believe I was an addict, (Which I will always be a recovering addict), but to make it so awful was he pretended that he knew all about it, but he actually didn't know about it. He never set foot in any of the homes I ever lived in and he never cared to take either of my kids to lunch or to a park. You know the usual things you see uncles and aunts do. They were too consumed in their lives—which is understandable—but my brother has a son, and I know he's had a few birthdays. Not once was I ever invited to my nephews birthday party. I would have been that aunt to spoil them rotten. What upsets me is when you pretend to know me, and when you never cared to have anything to do with me. Why do you have to go out of your way to try and tarnish my image? Truly, you don't have a clue as to who I am, and I will never give you the pleasure of getting to know me. You have lost that opportunity. I have tried many times to be a part of my own family, and the truth is no one puts in the effort. I'm sick of putting it in the effort alone. I want to live my life and start making my own friends, and create my own family. It's hard when you realize you don't matter to the ones you love the way they mattered to you. When my siblings had the opportunity to be good uncles and aunts, they didn't partake. Blood isn't thicker than water; it seems like, in my case, water is thicker than blood. Remember there is nothing wrong with you.

I had that urge to leave Weirdo in Georgia, but I chose to go and pick him up. I just wanted to take a shower in the hotel room, shave, and wash my clothes in the bathtub. Literally, I was in the hotel bathroom for four hours battling my thoughts, fears, and really just trying to figure out what my next move was going to be. I have always been told that in a relationship your partner should respect you. He should never hit you, and should always have your back, and correct you later behind closed doors if needed. It goes both ways. During my addiction, I battled with morality. I tried so hard to be moral and I held on to the little bit of dignity I thought I had. When you are actively using drugs—I hate to say this—it's impossible to live morally, and it was hard as hell to hold this persona that I was a decent human being to everyone when my mind was clouded and it was at war constantly with good and bad the entire time. It was so hard to balance addiction with morality. It was a job in itself. I excused Weirdo and my past behavior, and we made a vow that we would change and become better people for ourselves and for each other because we deserved it. During active addiction, I had a mouth on me, and as I have mentioned, addiction will not allow you under any circumstances to be in a good relationship. God will not allow it; it will be nothing but misery.

It's crazy because the more that I type or write, the more I find myself going back and realizing the growth, and learning where I stood at the time. I find the exact thing I went wrong, and the action I should have chosen to prevent things ending up the way they did. The main thing I'm trying to say is that drugs and alcohol will royally fuck up your life. Do not give up on life. We are fortunate and blessed to even be given the opportunity to walk on earth, and have lives. Let's make the best of our lives. God made our world amazing; it is what we choose to do with what God gifted us with that will determine whether or not this world goes to shit. Let's not take God and his gifts for granted.

So we made it to Dallas Texas, and I was reunited with my Unc. He filled me in with things that I needed to do since my father passed away. He said that I needed to get a passport and go to Egypt as soon as possible, because my brothers and my sisters were selling my father's property. He worked so hard for without getting my opinion about it, or including me. My Unc said this was meant for me, and to not let my brothers and my sisters rob me of my God given right. I was hurt, and went to messaging family members in Egypt to tell them not to sell anything, and that I planned on visiting Egypt soon.

Not once did any of my brothers and my sisters tell me anything about it. My brother was sending me 1,500.00 a month, which sucked because I wanted to invest in a home so that when I leave this world, I could leave something to my kids, and my brother had control over my share. Unc tried talking my brother into giving me all of my money. God and my father, who is watching me from heaven, knew I wasn't living right. My brother had no idea, and could really careless. After my brother and my sisters found out, I contacted my family in Egypt. They had literally cut me off from my inheritance, and my brother said it was because I was into drugs, but as I mentioned, my brother had no idea how I was living. He's always been the one to judge me by my past, when in actuality, his past is far worse than mine. I was lucky to never catch any charges. My records are clean, and so is Weirdo's. My brother has drug charges, speeding tickets, you name, it; he has a bad record. I have never judged him. I will let him think and continue to lie to the world and make himself think that he is and has always looked out for my best interest, but I'm tired of always having his back, and always sticking up for someone who really is a piece of shit for an individual. One of these days he's going to fall off of his horse, and I'm no longer going to be there to catch him.

This journey has taught me to stand up for myself, and to love me. I finally know how to love myself, and I'm finally able to truly love Weirdo for who he is, and appreciate all that he is. So the truth is my brother cut me off because I caught him and my siblings going behind my back to sell my father's property. In Egypt, my father worked so hard to leave his legacy, and I have ungrateful siblings that will never appreciate my father's hard work. So my brother cut me off to show how much control he had. I have been clean since July 4. It is my choice because I deserve to live. God pulled that money from me, and now that I'm clean and deserving of it, my brother would promise to send me the money the following week, and then a week later, he would tell me he didn't think I had learned my lesson. He never fulfilled his promise of sending me the money. I throw my hands up in the air. I accept the fact that I will never see my share, and my brother stole my inheritance, and it's ok, but God won't allow him to live a happy fulfilled true meaningful life until he changes his ways. I'm blessed for the first time in my life. I'm at peace with my spirit, and soul. I can bet you a million dollars. He is lost, and empty; he's done it to himself. I no longer feel sorry for him. I have faith that when all of this is over and done, I will come out victorious. God's got us. You just wait and see.

Before we left Dallas Texas, Unc told me not to worry, and that he loved me like he loved his own daughter. I'm putting my trust in that. I love him too, just like I love my Baba (means dad in Arabic).

Chapter 31

TRANSFORMATION

━━━━━

We left Dallas Texas, and Unc, and we made it to Austin Texas. This is where we have been for the past two months. Our Chevrolet Tahoe broke down. We have accepted the fact that we didn't just break down here for nothing; we broke down here for a reason, and this is where I finally figured out my purpose. Everything that is happening is necessary for our transformation. We have been sober since July 4, 2022, and we are stronger than ever. Spreading our gift, homeless, but grateful for this journey. It humbled us so much, and has us in love with each other and God to a point I never knew even existed.

We're figuring how to find shelter; they don't piss where they sleep. To my left there's a woman pouring her coffee into her Gatorade bottle. I don't blame her. A day in the life of the homeless you need fuel, and coffee is our crack, and at least this woman wasn't using drugs—from what i could tell she was sober, just mental. I was watching her apply her makeup, this bright red lipstick. I just knew if her hand slipped, it would get all over her teeth and it would be a disaster. I was watching her, watching everyone around us from the corner of her eyes. She was beautiful, and strong. She was posing with one hand holding on to a bike rack, her other hand on her hip. I'm not sure why she's dressed like that; the weather was extremely hot outside. She wore a hat like Hepburn. I caught myself muttering prayers for this woman. For some reason, I felt she needed protection.

Everyone started gathering up to get in line for coffee, and then we all would head into the First Methodist church for biscuits and gravy. Everyone was handed a different colored ticket. Mine was green, Weirdo's was orange, and when they called your color, you could get your food. My color was called first. There stood four elderly people on one side of this buffet serving us breakfast, and blessing us. You got three biscuits, three sausage patties, eggs, and sausage gravy. My God, it was an amazing experience. There was also a line for showers, but if you weren't at the church early enough, you couldn't make the list, and you didn't get a shower. Weirdo and I decided every Monday and Wednesday night we would sleep outside of the church so that we wouldn't miss the showers. They were real showers, not mobile showers like most places; they were clean and the water got hot, and stayed hot. The pavement and our sheet and pillow became best friends during those nights of the week.

I got my food. Weirdo's finally made it into the shower, and I sat at a table with this blond guy. He was perhaps in his late thirties. He was dressed in work clothes and painted all over his clothes. I greeted him, and he got up and walked away. Later on the same man and I had a conversation. He walked up to Weirdo and me, showing us this pocket knife he had, and was trying to sell it. His was name Bryan. Bryan said that's how he makes his beer money; he buys knives and sells them on the streets. I recognized the pocket knives because when I worked at a truck stop, we sold the same kind. He continued to tell us about another knife he had, and how the color of the handle was off a little and he sold it quickly. He said OCD had ruined every part of his life., because nothing seemed perfect to him anymore. He had lost his wife because he cheated on her. He was looking for something better. He lost his relationship with his kids because he couldn't accept them for who they were. He said OCD royally fucked him, so now he was homeless on the streets. He was an alcoholic, and he's constantly at war with himself in his head. God bless him.

In the beginning of this journey, we were quick to give our food away, to homeless people on the streets, but we learned quick that if we could get up every morning at the crack of dawn and get in line at a church or wherever to get fed, find a sidewalk to sleep on and not get robbed, or kicked off the premises, clothed, take showers, get bus passes, get a job and still be homeless and make it to work each day, even if it meant jumping in a swimming pool to get cleaned up before work, most of these people can do it. It's all about discipline. God wants us to be disciplined. That was something Weirdo and I weren't before this journey. Now we wake up at 3:30 a.m. every morning to get our day started, and we don't even need an alarm clock. All I'm trying to say is most of these people can. There are just a lot of lazy people, who are more than able to work, that gave up a long time ago. They would rather use drugs, and steal to make it. These types take advantage of phenomenal resources Austin Texas has to offer and ruin it for the people that are actually trying, but then you also have the mental, and elderly that are homeless; yet we don't mind helping them. Some of these elderly and mentally ill families don't even know they are out on the streets. Some are so old they don't even know how to communicate to anyone, and tell them how to reach their families. We learned quickly where to draw the line when it comes to helping people.

We slept in the pool chairs around the Laquinta hotel pool one night. We got woken up by the receptionist there and were made to leave, at least we got four hours of good sleep, if only we slept in the chairs closer to the office, so that when the receptionist looked out of the door, she would have stared straight and wouldn't have seen us. Nonetheless, we're just thankful we made it another day. Moreover, we would have missed breakfast at the Methodist Church, if we were not woken up. The only time we sleep past 3:30 a.m. was when we actually could find a comfortable spot, and we were left alone, but that was rare. Mosquitos have been the death of us, when we make it out of this state, we are going to buy hundreds of bottles of mosquito repellent and hand them out, because in the beginning of our journey, it seemed like any and everyone on the streets itched, scratched, and had blisters on their body. I judged, and automatically assumed they did drugs. You learn the difference quickly after you have walked in their shoes, and had to sleep outside every night while getting attacked by monster mosquitos.

"Emily you're the fucking reason I lost my home, you and your fucking police." This black homeless guy shouted as he was throwing chairs across the church cafeteria and exited the church. Accountability is a hard pill for a lot of the homeless to swallow, including myself. We're grateful to walk in the same shoes as all of the less fortunate, God made all of this necessary for our transformation. God is a genius. None of us are better than the other. We are all the same; we just struggle, and fight different battles and demons than others do. Everyone has a story, and should be heard, and not made to feel invisible.

I exited the church to go and smoke a cigarette, and outside of the church, I listened to two men talk, "Man do you have a *bowlo?*" One black male says to another. I think he was asking for a bowl, chalet, and glass pipe. That was what I called them or most meth heads in Alabama called them. I never heard of *bowlo*. And I was sure he was asking for dope. I'm pretty sure the other guy realized I was eavesdropping and decided to make a big deal out of it, and turn the heat from himself. So he went on to shout, "Don't be asking me for that. Just because I'm black doesn't mean I smoke dope, mother fucker." He went on to say, "Bitch, you're profiling me." Mind you these men were smart. They were quick to go from pissed to calm. The conversation was diverted to another homeless guy, and the two guys started talking about bicycles and how the tires were made in Germany. Here on the streets of Austin Texas, bikes to the homeless are like gold. You have to keep a close eye on them or else the dope dealer that sold it to you would steal it back and sell it to someone else, and the cycle repeats itself; it's crazy. Weirdo and I borrowed my boss' nephew's Schwinn bike; it was beautiful to door dash on and make some money for food, and everyone was checking the bike out. Weirdo and I would sleep with one hand through each tire. That was short-lived because we knew if the bike got stolen, we couldn't afford to pay it back at this time, so we returned the bike.

Chapter 32

SUMO COCAINE ADDICT

Just the other day we were at a bus stop, and this huge Asian American was laid out at the bus stop on the pavement in front of the bench. Weirdo and I were exhausted and decided to sit down on the bench. Walking all day will put a toll on you. This Asian dude was huge, and he reminded me of a sumo wrestler, but this dude grossed me the fuck out. He wouldn't stop sniffing, and hacking up shit, and spitting it not even a foot away from where we sat. "Are you the police?" Sumo said to Weirdo, and Weirdo responded, "Nope." Sumo proceeded to pour a white substance out of a bag onto his wallet on the pavement right in front of us. Back in the day I snorted some lines of cocaine, but never as much as Sumo was about to do right in front of us. I knew Weirdo and I thought about the same thing every time we looked over at each other. (Why is this dumbass snorting this shit right in front of us, sweating balls? There's absolutely nothing cool about it. In fact, it was annoying as fuck). I mean it was disgusting. When our bus finally pulled up, Weirdo and I literally shouted with joy; we were saved from Sumo. Now that I look back, I ask myself if God was showing us this to remind us why we don't ever have to get back into that lifestyle. I truly believe God was.

"I gotta make sure you're really here." "I'm really here," said Weirdo, looking back at me, with the most beautiful green eyes I fell in love with every day. I had to squeeze his hand a little harder, just to make sure. We were walking down the sidewalk, headed to the Trinity center, another church that helped the state of Austin Texas. We were going to check and see if we had any mail to pick up. We also needed to charge our cell phones. It's hard to find an outlet when you're homeless, without getting kicked out of establishment after establishment because you're not a paying customer.

"Did you guys make breakfast?" Shouted our friend, Michael. He always showed up at the right time. He is probably in his late sixties, a great spirit. He's homeless. Strangely, every time I see him, he's clean cut, well groomed, and never looks distressed. One of these days, I'll get his story. He was always telling us what church to go to for food, bus passes, showers, and all the other resources around. I call him archangel Michael because to me he always came bearing good news. He is a very peaceful man.

There was a time I wanted to confront this duche, for the way he was treating this younger kid. I wasn't quite sure why this younger kid (male) was taking a shower

There was a time I wanted to confront one guy on the way he was treating a younger kid. I was surprised to see he was taking his shower across from me in the women's bathroom, when only women were supposed to be in there. I felt extremely uncomfortable because he was done with his shower and walked out of the stall butt ass naked. I was hiding behind my shower curtain waiting patiently for him to leave. Why wasn't this kid taking a shower in the men's bathroom? He must have feared something, and felt safe in the women's restroom. About two days later, I saw this young boy walking down the street with this black male probably in his late sixties holding an umbrella over the man's head. Not even a week before the same young boy was tagging along with this old white male, probably in his early seventies. The old man would shout out to the kid and tell him to round him up a cigarette, and the boy would jump up quickly and do as he was told. There has just been a very uneasy feeling about this entire situation. I felt like I bit my tongue long enough. So indirectly I was going to ask this black man why all the homeless men treated this young boy like garbage—like he was their bitch, or slave, When I was about to question this guy on why he was mistreating this boy, archangel Michael appeared and cut in and said, "Excuse me but did you make it to Saint Vincent church for lunch?" He bedded in so quickly. I knew he saved me from unnecessary conflict. I've got to remember to pick my battles wisely, because not all battles are worth fighting. It's just so hard for me to sit back and watch something go on that I know in my heart is not right. I pray for that boy every day, and when I see him in the streets, I feel his pain; he's losing it, and you can look into his eyes and see emptiness. Feeling something extremely hard to deal with kills me inside, knowing people are suffering, and they feel alone. Where is the love? Where is the unity? Why are people taking this beautiful planet for granted?

I looked at Weirdo and that man's smile; my man's smile was so big. I whispered, "Archangel Michael" into Weirdo's ear, and Weirdo winked at me. There is hope, and we are protected. Everything I ever dreamed of in a man, Weirdo was becoming since childhood. It's amazing what God's doing with us.

Chapter 33

CHEVY TAHOE

───────

"Thank you God" both Weirdo and I jumped for joy. Our Chevrolet Tahoe was still safely parked and not towed. We literally started laughing and couldn't stop grinning. God was taking care of us without a doubt. Just sitting in my Tahoe, yes it was still broken, but just appreciating the fact that it's ours and we still have it. God has been listening to your cries and prayers. Weirdo and I checked on the Tahoe for an entire week because we knew there wasn't anything we would do financially. Moreover, we were scared we would get there and it would be gone. Our hearts couldn't take much more heartache. We grabbed some clothes and our pillows, and went on our way.

Our truck has been parked behind a junk yard in little Texas, and south congress, for the past two months. It is in a public parking lot so every day we fear that the truck will be impounded and it will bring us further cost, and it will be impossible for us to come up with the money to retrieve it from the impound. Or someone on the Austin Texas Mutual aid site will contact me and lie to me, and give me false hope and tell us he's going to give us and install a transmission from a truck he owns but instead he would be plotting to steal our Cadillac converter. I've reached out to get help, and have had many broken promises. Something by this time I'm extremely used to. All we want to do is get our truck fixed, travel the rest of the world, find my mom, tell her I love her before she grows older and forgets me, and continue spreading sobriety and God. We want to see the world; we have been through hell and back and refused to be chained down anymore. I want to give hope to everyone that's lost home and needs a little nudge.

Chapter 34

GAY PRIDE IN AUSTIN TEXAS

"What's it like to live with two pussies?" We heard from around the corner we were grabbing some coffee and spending money that neither of us needed to spend, but we needed to treat ourselves every now and again. We were both curious and eager to find out what the commotion was about. We stumbled across a drag queen show. G.g. SuperNova was the host to this wedding gig they were having at the Sheraton hotel—a really nice hotel. Her voice is the voice we heard and it was so audible; we could hear it at the Starbucks.

Personally, she was gorgeous. The perfect jet black bun, black and white leotard, and that drag queen could shake it better than most women I had seen. The gay men here danced better than women too. They were doing cartwheels, splits, and all I could wonder was how their junk was doing, because to me they weren't supposed to physically be able to do such things without physically hurting themselves. I know that shit hurts. "Skinny bitches," the queen bee the host wouldn't quit shouting. This lifestyle was amazing. I got the queen b's autograph, on the original notebook paper this book was journaled in. Plus a few of the other autographs from some other drag queens. We told the queen bee about the journey we were on and she literally got on her microphone and congratulated us on our sobriety and wished us luck to the entire audience. It was encouragement that we needed to hear. I was filled with a weird kind of joy, and I cried. It was a cry of joy, a feeling of accomplishment, a nudge to keep on going.

Maxine walked out on the stage, and she was this voluptuous beautiful woman, well man, and her theme went out to all the gentlemen. She sang: "You can jump on me, and ride my ass. I don't care how you fuck me; just fuck me right, and right now." She went on, "Need you to fuck me; you're necrophilia, and I just died. You can fuck me in the Pakistan, and hold my pussy up like the Taliban." Weirdo and I laughed so hard. We were excited to celebrate Austin Gay pride for free with the drag queens. I told Weirdo, "I bet no one in Alabama got to experience what we just did." The show went on, "My ass is fat, and my pussy is foul. Fuck Brad Abbot; black lives matter." We had so much fun, but that had to end and we had a journey to continue. It felt good to take a break from the everyday worries of everything, but as this journey goes on, you will learn that we learn to appreciate the tiny things, and we begin to evolve into beautiful people.

Chapter 35

MY DRINK, GOT GOT

We went on our way, "Hey didn't you just have a drink?" Weirdo asked me, and I looked both ways. I had just placed my cup on top of a newspaper machine. We had been delayed for two minutes from the bus headed to the plasma center to donate. Then Weirdo pointed at this black kid walking up the road. He was speed walking up the road, swaying back and forth with my big gulp happy as can be. "Hey that's my drink," I yelled out facing the direction the kid was joyfully walking while drinking my drink. He looked back finally, placed my drink in the middle of the road about 100 feet away from Weirdo and me, and kept going. Our bus driver got back on the bus and I felt I won't have time to make it back on the bus if I decided to go after my drink. I was just shocked because I literally placed my drink down, and it was gone in the blink of an eye.

We finally made it to the plasma center and were turned away because here in Austin Texas the homeless aren't allowed to donate, just in case a blood test comes back negative and they need to reach the homeless. We walked out the plasma center and the heat put me in this shitty ass mood, plus not being able to get the $100.00.God knew we needed to put toward the transmission, but everything that's happening is necessary, and God wants us here a bit longer. We still have a lot to learn.

Yep my punk ass took my anger out on Weirdo. He didn't deserve it, but being on the streets has put a toll on Weirdo and me. I later apologized to him. Weirdo and I started getting sleepy and found an unoccupied house we decided to sleep in the driveway. We literally laid our sheet in the middle of the driveway, so that everyone in the neighborhood could see we weren't trying to break into the residents; we were just trying to find somewhere safe to sleep. We didn't get but two hours of sleep.

The neighbors across the street literally were fighting like cats and dogs. It reminded Weirdo and I how much we appreciate sobriety, and how we don't miss fighting the way we used to, it reminded us so much of us back in Alabama. God was reminding us every day, to keep doing good, and to not back track because we didn't want to relive the lifestyle we were fortunate to witness everyday while living on the street. Mosquitos though, we learned really fucking quick to stock up on mosquito spray, otherwise there would be no sleep in Austin Texas, at least not on these streets.

I'm only human; it's hard to live on these streets. I don't know how these addicts and alcoholics are surviving out here, and they must be at a complete mental war with themselves

24/7. God bless them. We want to help people, but a lot of people out here are not helping themselves. Sadly they have become complacent, and to me many are lazy and ungrateful.

They choose this lifestyle. So we learned who to help, and who to avoid. I am starting to think God is giving us a second chance to write our wrongs, and it's your choice to continue going astray, or grasp the opportunity, and start living right. We made it back on the bus, headed back to Republic Square, to figure out what bus to take to get to Sunrise Church. I was staring out through the bus window, before the it pulled off. I saw a black male, perhaps in his mid-forties looking through this trash can and pulled out a twisted lemonade can. It looked empty, but the man proceeded to sip out of the can. His arm was up, and he looked like a dinosaur, pterodactyl, because of the way he was holding his arms. Honestly, it looked as if he were drawing and the nerves in his arms were quenching up. "Bless him," I muttered under my breath, and tears started falling from my eyes. I was where he was at, at a time in my life, just not as bad, and I began to pray and Thank God for the protection He had given me throughout my life, because things could have been a lot worse for me. I'm just grateful that Weirdo and I are still sober. Yes, I still throw my brat fits, and yes, he still takes it and yes we continue to evolve into beautiful human beings.

Chapter 36

CAT AND MOUSE

"Wake up", you guys can't sleep here; it's too open. The cops will be here and you don't want to go to jail. I'm sorry guys I know it's like cat and mouse out here. If you want to get some sleep you have to hide." Weirdo and I wiped the sleep from our eyes. We've already woken up from beneath some stairs of an emergency exit in a parking garage. It was rough; there were cobwebs all under the stairs. Weirdo and I sprayed mosquito repellant all over our bodies. There was caca smeared on the wall right next to where Weirdo was laying. I held him close to me so he wouldn't accidentally brush up against it. The previous day, we walked into a job, (we won't disclose) and I got offered a two day trial run where I was paid $**.** an hour for four hours for two days, and on the third day, if my performance was satisfactory, I would be hired for $1.00 more an hour, and if I made it through the first three days, I would get a $100.00 bonus. I don't think they thought I was going to make it. The first two days of work I got paid in cash, while living on the street. A hotel room, and a good shower and meal was what I treated Weirdo and myself to.

We managed to spend the night right outside of the First Methodist Church. We knew we couldn't miss the biscuits and gravy, and the free showers that they offered. I'm not even going to lie; we got geeked up at 5 a.m. coffee, tore up the biscuits and gravy, socialized with a few of our fellow homeless friends, which honestly they are becoming family.

We decided to catch the 801 bus to another church called St. Vincent; we got there at 7:50 a.m. The line doesn't start until 9:30 am. Weirdo out in the cold, and even if I tried to go back to sleep while we waited for the church to open the coffee wouldn't allow it. I'm excited for what God had planned for us. I pray for patience. That's the hardest thing for me to deal with right now; it's something I continue to learn. Everything works out just perfectly, because if I would have settled with dominoes sit would have only paid $****, which is a lot less than I knew I deserved, and God blessed me with patience for the job that I have now. I can't stress this enough. I am proud of what the two of us are becoming as a team, truly, and I know for a fact he's my soul mate. We both for once are on the same page; we want to take care of each other, and we would do anything to keep each other safe. We're building a foundation, one that after all of these years, it seems like many lifetimes we deserve. We are each other's family, and I wouldn't change it for the world.

We both sat up. It's about that time for the line to start flowing and people entering the building. I leaned over Weirdo's tummy writing in my notebook as he was knocked out asleep; it always made me feel better knowing that he was getting some sleep. We got up and made it to some free bus passes and a $10.00 H.E.B. gift card. Ask and you will receive; God provides.

Narrators insert:

I hope you all are learning. I know I have. God has truly freed us from the chains of Satan. We are finally getting what we deserve; we are learning how to live. We love helping people, and loving everyone. In the beginning of this journey, I didn't like people. I didn't even like myself. God is a genius. We did not break down in Austin Texas by accident.

Chapter 37

TWENTY-NINE AND DYING

I was eavesdropping and overheard a young man named Josh, who is terminal with stage four cancer. He has a beautiful dog. It breaks my heart thinking he doesn't have long life to live. All I could think about was why? Why so young, and where is the dog going to go when Josh eventually passes away. The dog would be so heart-broken and it was going to break my heart. The way Josh continues on with his life not giving up and just fighting through it, makes me proud of this young man. Josh mentioned he wants to make it to Colorado; he was describing three little waterfalls he wants to get to. I hope he makes it.

Another man goes on to speak about how his lungs just stop whenever they feel like it, then start back up. He said God told him He has seven years left to live, and he's going to make the best of it. He wants to move to a farm, buy two cats and two dogs, and let them grow up together. The different dreams from these random strangers give us hope in humanity. As I've said before, you are in control of your own paradigm. Don't listen to what everyone else says.

Narrators insert:

Situations such as these have opened my eyes, and taught me to appreciate life, because tomorrow isn't promised.

Chapter 38

OFFICIALLY A UHAUL EMPLOYEE

━━━━━

Going through all the tires in the abandoned truck was depressing, because I found a diploma, a graduation cap and gown, some family pictures that I couldn't bring myself to throw away, and the property belonged to the delinquent renter. Weirdo and I left all of our memories behind and it made me think, *I wonder if my landlord felt the same way about our things when she was cleaning out our old trailer.* Anyways that's in the past and I know God wants me to leave it there.

I know nothing is coincidental, what are the chances that I land a job with good people. I'm able to set up camp right next to my job, and have a job that throws out some of the most useful things that employees get to keep, such as furniture, game systems, clothes, jewelry. Weirdo and I got a futon mattress that fits perfectly in our tent with pillows and a BAUX neck fan you wear around your neck to keep you cool, which honestly I think my coworkers bought for us, and pretended it was left in the truck; it was brand new. Or maybe God just knew what we needed. We took it all as a blessing, and it was. The Lord always provides. It gets hot as hell in our tent. The best part about all of this is whatever we don't need Weirdo and I can take it to all the homeless camps and distribute it to all the homeless—which makes our hearts sing. Moreover, it will give us incentive to talk to everyone and maybe get through to some of these homeless people and get them on the right track, at least give them some hope.

I was ready to go to Walmart, and buy 100 notebooks, pens, panties for the woman and feminine products, and get out on the streets and hand them all out. I've had to roll toilet paper from a gas station to make a maxi pad, and literally, every single time I did, I had a huge blood stain in my pants by the end of the day. It's not fun. I was super excited to blow my money on every homeless person out there, and not once did I think about Weirdo, and my situation. We ended up taking my money and buying a tent, tarp, bug spray. These are the necessities if you're going to live on the street. "Narcy, we just got kicked out of our spot," Weirdo said as I was alighting from a truck. I just got through parking a 20 foot returned truck at my work. My eyes filled up with tears, but I know I've got to keep it together. During times like this, I want to question God, but I know better. I go on to tell Weirdo to just pack our stuff up and leave it to God. This is confirmation that God sent Weirdo to me to protect me because I couldn't handle getting kicked out by myself. It would have really just fucked me up. Weirdo has always been my protector; he's always taken care of the dirty work. Hopefully one day, I'll be able to carry some of the load. I love this man.

I still had about two hours left before I got to clock out and leave work. I made it. I clocked out, and walked to meet Weirdo and we would figure out together what our next move was going to be. Every day I am learning to love, respect, and appreciate Weirdo more, Gods blessed me with an angel. Weirdo and I had to leave our mattress behind; it was too much to tote. I knew Weirdo wanted to cry but he held it together. I'm so proud of him. We came across an apartment complex and saw a maintenance closet, figured we could put both suitcases in it so that we wouldn't look homeless and we could literally take baths in their swim pool, when no one was looking, and that's exactly what we did. I had a bar of zest soap we got from one of these churches in a care package. The pool looked pretty murky, so Weirdo and I figured we would do them a favor and zestfully clean it. I think living on the streets I managed to keep myself cleaner than when I actually had my home and a shower to bathe. I always had this fear that I was going to let myself go and start smelling like urine and caca like a lot of the homeless people do sadly. God bless them all.

Chapter 39

WE MET AN ANGEL

Every now and again Weirdo and I would have these crazy spurts of wanting to door dash on foot. We got hungry! We managed taking a door dash order and attempting to walk 2.4 miles to get there. We were starving and at that point we were going to once again make the impossible possible. The customer ended up canceling their order before we made it to deliver their food. I'm sure we took too long. It's hard to keep a phone charged when you're homeless, and documenting everything and posting it on the internet, in hopes to help people make better choices in their lives. We got to eat the order. I swear it was probably the best two steak tacos we ever ate in our entire lives. I'm probably just saying that because we were starving. We got up and began walking until we came across this place called Texas Chili Parlor, where we sat on some stairs right across from it. We decided this to be the perfect time to draw signs to panhandle, and as we both started writing on our signs, a man walked up to us. He was limping on a cane, wearing a trench coat and a hat with a drawstring in the front under his chin, and a mask. The first thing he said was, "I love you," and gave me dap and then turned to Weirdo and said, "I love you," and gave him dap. This man was called Angel. We explained to him that this journey is teaching us how to take responsibility for our past selfish ways. Accountability is a hard pill to swallow. It's amazing how everything works itself out.

This entire journey has literally been a phenomenon, a divine intervention, a healing that I hope everyone gets the privilege to experience one day. We explained that we had been given the best gift ever and that it is sobriety as well as a clear head and the ability to walk in shoes less fortunate than us. Angel asked to see our marker and asked if he could sit down and draw with us; of course, we invited him with welcoming arms. Angel started to draw, then he would hand the card board over to Weirdo, and then it would be my turn. Every time Angel drew, he would say, "Just look, just look," and then he would remind us that he loved us. The three of us continued to draw together, as we drank out of the same big cup of water I got from inside the Texas chili parlor. Every so often Angel would start crying, and I would ask him why he was crying and he would point up at the sky and say, "Cristol," (Which means Jesus Christ in Spanish). He said God did all of this for us, and we would start crying tears of joy with him. We completely forgot we were making signs to pan handle.

Angel would have random spurts of mixed emotions. He would laugh with tears streaming down his face, and then he would cry and say they were tears for God. I continued to offer him water because by this time the three of us had been outside for at least three hours. Our cardboard started looking like a masterpiece.

We ended up making friends with a young woman from the parlor. She would sneak outside to smoke a cigarette every chance she got, and Angel would start flirting with her in an innocent and humorous way. He really took a liking to this young lady. Her name was Atila, and she was a feisty straight to the point type of girl. The first thing she said to Weirdo and I was, "What can I do for you?" And is this guy giving you problems?" She was talking about Angel. I'm sure she thought he was some drunk bum, but we were quick to say, "NO," she walked back into work and Angel said, "If she comes back outside she better have eaten a steak, fried chicken, and some potato chips or else she's not coming home with me." I mean the three of us laughed so hard and it was a real laugh—you know, the type that makes you cry, your chest hurts and you almost pee on yourself, that kind of laugh exactly.

I could see this Amazing glow in Weirdo's face, a glow that made me adore this Peter Pan, innocent, child-like being that I once treated so badly. My father used to jokingly flirt with women just like Angel was doing, and it used to crack my brothers and sisters up. The older we got, the more embarrassing it became. The last time I laughed so hard it was with my father. This happened many years ago. My eyes kept filling up with tears. These were tears of joy, and some tears I couldn't explain. I felt like my father was with us.

It started to get late in the evening, probably around 7 pm. The sky was filled with some of the most beautiful purple, pinks, and blues. The sun was full and gorgeous and Weirdo and I had never actually watched a sunset. Angel started playing music on his cell phone. He played real Mexican music, and would sing along and make us watch the YouTube video with him, and we would continue to laugh. Strangely, the second song angel played for us was Mariah Carrey's son, "Oh when you walk by every night, talking sweet and looking fine." I'm sure everyone knows what song I'm talking about with just those lyrics, but it's strange to me before Weirdo and I were sitting on the pavement at a bus stop humming the exact song angel played, and for the life of us we couldn't figure out the lyrics, or who sang it, but this stranger was playing it on YouTube for us in Spanish, and this was all the confirmation we needed. Both Weirdo and I knew Angel was in fact an Angel.

Hold on, it gets better. Your father absolutely loved Mexican food. When I was younger, until two years ago when he passed away, our whole family would go and eat at this Mexican restaurant, and my father would walk in, and automatically start joking around, speaking complete gibberish and I mean my father was such a comedian. None of us knew what he was saying but all the Mexicans would laugh so hard and my father became a fixture at this Mexican restaurant, they treated our family like family.

The crazy thing about all of this is, when I was in active addiction, I built this ugly hate for Mexicans for no reason. I mean, I was racist toward them, and I had no idea why. Now that I look back I believe the devil was trying his hardest to distance me more and more from my father, and that was a way to do it. The more we got to know Angel, the more I saw my father (actual dad) in him. He had the same eyes as my dad. I began crying every time angel cried.

Out of nowhere angel looked at weirdo and said, "You don't need to get jealous. Narcy is a very special girl, a very good girl," he told Weirdo. "Narcy chose you, and only you, you are hers, and she's yours," but no matter what you do, never get jealous. She picked you, and you are very special to her. The three of us were still sitting on these stairs right across from the parlor, and Angel pointed at Weirdo and me. He looked straight ahead. There were two skyscrapers and right dab in the center of these two skyscrapers we saw the most beautiful sun set, and it was setting directly on us and in front of us. The most beautiful shades of purple and pink are my favorite colors. The three of us had tears streaming down our cheeks, and right dab in the middle of the sunset was a power pole in the shape of a cross. It was extraordinary. Nothing's a coincidence. What were the chances that the three of us would be at that exact spot, at that exact moment praising God, confessing our sins, and giving the Lord up above a thanks that we now know it's impossible to thank the Lord enough.

We began to wrap things up. Angel looked at me, and said, "It's hard to look at you, your eyes, you have the same eyes as my friend Debbie." It was obvious Debbie played a big part in Angel's life. As we began to hug and bid our farewells, Angel held my hand, and I asked him, "Will we ever see you again?" and he replied, "Not in this lifetime, but I promise we will meet again in the next lifetime." We wouldn't let go of each other's hands. I swear my father was with us that night. He told Weirdo he wanted to see us walk away, so Weirdo and I held hands and we began to walk away. I was balling at this point, but with the biggest smile on my face. I looked at Weirdo and told him, "That was my father." I finally got the approval from my father, the man (Weirdo), that I'm deeply learning to love and I'm falling more and more in love with, every time I look at him. All I ever wanted was my father's approval, and I truly believe that I just got it. My father got to tell his baby girl goodbye, and this girl finally made her father proud. He watched his first born daughter walk away with the third love of her life—my father being the first of course, then my son, and then Weirdo.

Narrators insert:

Ever since this incident happened, Weirdo and I have still been broken down, homeless, sober, grateful, and understanding of why everything that is occurring is necessary for our growth, and it's all part of the divine intervention God has planned for us. We didn't break down in Austin Texas by accident. During this stay here in Austin Texas, we have yet to run into Angel. He did say that we wouldn't see him in this lifetime again, but he promised to see us again in the next lifetime. Can't a living soul ever make me question God's existence again? We all heartedly believe, and we have a lot of work to do.

Chapter 40

RECAP

This chapter gives a brief recap. Weirdo said God sent him to me; both Weirdo and I have tattoos on us of the number 13. Weirdo got his tattoo when he was in a band with his brother called, "The Redroom," and they were going to do something different every 13th track. Weirdo's adventure was going to be the first 13 track on their first album, and I got mine one night when I was downtown Columbus Ga. With income tax money I didn't know what to do with it. Lil Baghdad's birthday fell on the 13th, and he will always have the biggest part of my heart; he's no longer with us anymore. Weirdo and I have a scar on our foreheads from childhood, and were both allergic to penicillin. Literally, every time my leg falls asleep so does his. He completes my thoughts, and vice versa. Both of us know what each other is thinking before words even leave our mouths. Both of us have brothers that supposedly committed suicide. Strangely, when I get cuts or scratches, he has marks in the same exact spots as me. As a little girl, I imagined my prince charming looking exactly like Weirdo; it scares the shit out of me, his height,, his eyes, his hair, his torso, his facial structure, everything! It scares the shit out of me. He's my soulmate, my protector, and my angel. God is a genius. We met Angel on August 13, 2022... Tell me this is a coincidence, and I'll look at you like you're crazy.

Chapter 41

NOT BY COINCIDENCE

Weirdo and I were determined to help people even around my job, plus we were still waiting at the Trinity center to get his birth certificate in the mail Iris. This was on one of the two days that I was off at Uhaul. I had my license and my social security card, and I did my application. Weirdo didn't have his license or any of that but they needed help at one of the construction sights and asked both of us to be there in the morning. There was a big possibility that they would send us out. Weirdo from Muscogee county, it was really strange to me because we had already put in for his birth certificate but we put it in Lee county and that's not where Weirdo was born; we learned that a little later. He had no idea where he was born. His mother got him and his brother's birthplace confused, which is weird because at times I confuse the two birthplaces of both my children, but that's part of my alcohol and drug use. Thank God for sobriety. I am clear headed and my memories are coming back.

For people that are reading this and live in Austin Texas, the Trinity center is one of the many establishments that help the homeless; you can get a picture ID, and a social security card at the center. So Weirdo and I decided to walk for a bit, and we came across a staffing agency called Pacesetters. If you are physically able to work you need to. Idle minds are the devil's playground. I'm super excited that I was actually able to use that phrase. I'm a nerd, I know.

So we decided to walk for a bit, and we came across a staffing agency called pacesetters. We met a female named Lilly. This was on one of the two days that I had my social security card. Robert didn't have his license or any of that but they needed help at one of the construction sights and asked us to be there the following morning. There was a possibility that they would send us out. Robert and I decided we would go and get some pizza from the seven eleven and find a place to sleep. We came across a nice apartment complex with a parking garage at this time. We needed a shower too, so we had learned to quit being bashful, and every time someone came up to the main entrance, we would ask them if they would use their key to let us in the pool entrance for us to take a dip and get cleaned up. At least three of the tenants just walked by and ignored us. We got our feelings hurt and just gave up. We ended up being full from our pizza, and falling asleep right next to the entrance of the apartment complex. We were woken up by this white male, probably in his mid-twenties, screaming, "You all need to get your fucking asses up. You all can't sleep out here." He had his dog right up on us. He was a really nice dog and didn't behave like his owner. Robert and I tried getting up but the guy was literally in our get up space, and we had no room to stand up.

At this time I had enough with being homeless and being treated like wild animals by a lot of people who in all honestly acted like wild animals. I was fed up and so was Weirdo.

I couldn't bite my tongue anymore. There was another tenant watching this entire incident from the side. She was probably in her early sixties, blonde hair, and somewhat rock star looking. She seemed scared and didn't want to get involved. I stood up for what I knew was right, "Dude you don't know where we have come from, you don't know what we have been through." I went to say, "I don't give a fuck."

"You're a fucking whore, and he's a fucking crack head. You need to get the fuck off my property before I call the cops," he yelled.

Right then and there I knew he was under the influence of something. The kid screwed up when he made me cry. That was Robert's last straw; he would literally die for me. That's a wonderful feeling, not that he would die, but that after all these years going through all the things I have been through, I finally got that protector I had wished for my entire life. It's a good feeling knowing someone genuinely has your back, and I have his back no matter what; he's my protector. Robert flung his coffee at the guy. I'm proud of Weirdo. The way the kid was acting he should have really beat the hell out of him. I was holding him back and the kid was antagonizing the hell out of us; he kept getting literally an inch in our face. The kid tried recording us on YouTube, and telling us that he was going to share with the world that this crack ass bum flung coffee on him. The kid asked for it, and finally the cops arrived. Right before the cops had arrived, Weirdo kept telling me to come on because this guy was not worth our time and needed to go before we ended up going to jail for something we didn't deserve—just like when we were in Dallas Texas.

Remember that the devil is real, and he really does work through people. The devil was working through this cop, as he was working through this kid that kicked us out of the apartment complex. But the guy failed to mention when the police arrived that he had threatened us with a gun and a knife, and this was all because we were sleeping at this apartment complex entrance where it was well lit, and we wouldn't be woken up by someone kicking our heads in and stealing our shit. It's crazy because it seemed the spot we chose became more dangerous than sleeping outside of the Capital with all the other homeless people. Where is the love y'all?

The cops got there, and I was firm with my beliefs and stronger than ever. I wasn't going to budge until I spoke up for both Weirdo and me and I was shaking so badly. I was just so upset; this kid really had no idea what we had been through, and how hard this journey really was. The rockstar looking chick was just around the corner observing everything; she actually came and talked to the cop on our behalf. The cops told me to calm down and sit down. Then he proceeded to talk to the belligerent kid, and the kid literally yelled at the cop and told him, "I called you, why are you siding with them?" Then the kid told the cop, "You seem a little stressed out but do your job, and put them in jail." The cop did almost the complete opposite, and almost threw his ass in jail. Robert and I got up and brushed it off and literally looked at each other and knew God was looking out for us. God never fails us. Man, I'm on a roll. I want to continue typing but I need to get to work. I will continue later. God bless everyone. It really gets better.

I'm actually at work typing now, and I am grateful to be here. The previous day my boss told me that I was not leaving Austin Texas till after March. When I asked him the reason, he said at the end of March. Literally, that knot in the back of my throat was there again. I wanted to cry. Robert and I want to see the rest of the United States. We have been in this box our entire lives, and we truly believe our spirits yearn for it. I want to hang out with my biological mother. I want to make her dreams come true, because I know as a mother, I'm not being involved in my kids' life. I wish I could be. So 37 years later, my mom deserves it; she's suffered long enough. My boss even said that if it meant I would return to work at his Uhaul, he would go with me to meet my mother.

Chapter 42

PIZZA AND TAZ

We managed to find this gazebo with outlets right next to Texas University. The security guards don't mess with you here. In fact, there's a maintenance man that looks out for the homeless. This is where we met our friend Taz, the young fellow we turned on to rehab. Bless his heart you would have to meet him for yourself. I promise you would fall in love with him, just like we did. Right before we were able to contact a treatment facility for Taz, he took his chalet (glass pipe), smashed it in a towel, and before he showed it to us, he asked us if we were triggered by anything and at first we didn't realize what he was talking about, and realized once he opened the towel up on our picnic table under the gazebo. He was so excited to show us he crushed all his dope and paraphernalia in a towel. I literally started sharing tears of joy. I was so proud of this young man; all he needed was a little push, and we were that push.

Taz went on to pull out seven dollars and asked me if I would pick him up for some breakfast pizza because I was already going to the seven eleven to pick up some coffee. You guys know me by now; coffee is my best friend, and I told Taz sure. So I left Taz and Robby at the gazebo, got on my bike (and mind you I'm still an amateur on my bike), and rode up hills. Honestly, I got off my bike and walked up that hill. My legs aren't as floppy and weak as they used to be; riding bikes has literally woken up some muscles that my body forgot it even had.

When I got to the seven eleven, sadly they didn't have breakfast pizzas, and I was just still super excited with the progress we were having with Taz. I'm determined to get this young man pizza. It was probably about 9 in the morning. I saw that there was a Domino's pizza right next door to this seven eleven, and I thought to myself there's no way it was open. Then I saw that there was this young lady sitting in her van right outside of the Domino's pizza, so I decided to talk to her. She was a free spirit, just very friendly, and someone I felt comfortable talking to instantly. I told her why I was around. I refused to give up, just like I didn't want Taz giving up, on what this is becoming a journey for him—a journey hopefully that will change his life for the good forever, that chance I believed he deserved. I was going to make sure he succeeded. It was another one of those making the Impossible Possible.

Of course I had a deep conversation with this young lady (when I say I had this currency, I mean the gap never stops when I get excited about this, and anything I'm passionate about). This is where my heart is. This is my soul's purpose, Thirty seven years in and this girl finally finds her purpose. The young lady at Domino's blessed me with over 20 pizzas from the night before—she was going to have to throw them away—some of them were burnt but most of them weren't. I parked my bike inside of the establishment as took eight boxes of pizza, wings, cheese bread; you name it, and returned to the gazebo. I knew the woman would take care of my bike. She had a story to tell, and she started from the beginning, and yes she was working at Domino's. I could tell she didn't find her soul's purpose and that didn't mean she won't get there; it probably just took me giving her that little nudge she needed. I encouraged her to not settle, and to find what makes her truly happy in life.

When I was descending down the hill, Taz and Weirdo saw me struggling with these eight boxes, and run to me to help. The smiles on their faces were priceless. I mean even when we are homeless, we are happy and trying to shine our light on everyone around us; we make the best out of all situations.

The young lady at Domino's and I became good friends and I got the boys so that they could help me. I'm sure she really just wanted to meet the people I was telling her about, who wouldn't. Of course I told the boys the deal, and they were ready to go back with me, but I had to remind them that we were just blessed and we didn't want to get greedy, and lose our future blessings. I think the boys and I really just wanted to get more pizza so that we could take them to as many homeless people we could come across, but we ended up not going back, because after we ate we were full. Thank God, and just wanted to sleep. I know we can get pizza from Domino's anytime my friend is working. That's one thing about Austin Texas; you never go hungry. God always provides.

Chapter 43

C. WILLIAMS

So I work every day of the week except for Monday and Tuesdays, and Weirdo door dashes for our cigarettes, food, and hygiene money while I'm at work. I can honestly say he has met a few interesting characters, and immediately I return from work, he's beyond excited to tell me all about them. I'm skeptical, at times. I worry about Weirdo when he's out and about because he is naive to a lot of things. His discernment needs some work. I'm always the one to be like, "Hold on Weirdo, let's think about this," and I get him to understand situations. I'll share a brief story with you after we talk about our dear friend C. Williams. As I mentioned in the beginning of my book, Weirdo is like Peter Pan. He has innocence about him, he reeks of it, everyone catches on to it, and they take advantage of him. I try to catch people before it happens, and I have to say I told you so, but he's getting better, I'll admit.

Well, Weirdo once told me he made a friend at the bus stop and spent a lot of time with him that day. I had a great day at work that day, so I was eager to learn about him. He approached me like a little kid, and I listened to him. Coincidentally, C. Williams was sitting at the bus stop where we were going to have to go to get to our destination. I honestly couldn't tell you where we were going. All I know is I met C. and he's another one that I absolutely fell in love with.

Chris looked exactly like Val Kilmer, for those of you that don't know who he is, he's an amazing actor. He played a role in "The Doors, Batman Forever, and Tombstone." I think he even played a role in "Top Gun," if I'm not mistaken." I mean he looked like he should be in a movie. He had some of the most beautiful blue eyes that I had ever seen. These beautiful blue eyes were some of the most tired and lonely eyes I had ever seen. This man wanted to tell me his story. I'm pretty sure he was sick and tired of being sick and tired of the lifestyle he was living. God bless him. You know this is just confirmation once again that Weirdo did not meet this man by accident; nothing happens coincidentally. It's becoming more and more clear the longer we are in Austin Texas that we aren't here by accident; we're here to help heal the forgotten, and the lost out here. We're just like them, and not any better.

We were fortunate enough to be trusted to record Chris's story, and we will treasure this new friendship for the rest of our lives. Chris is a full blown alcoholic. Weirdo and I were full blown alcoholics not while we were dating but at times in our lives, which helps us relate to C. This recording is when I realized I wanted to make a documentary because we all have stories that must be shared.

Weirdo's insert:

I would just like to add that while I was an alcoholic I remember waking up in a ditch on the side of the road a few times, passed out in my own urine and vomited, and would also just be looking for a fight so I got kicked out of every bar I ever went to drink. I was still in high school, and would always miss school. I remember my first sip of alcohol was a shot of Jim Beam whiskey. I don't remember how old I was but maybe 12 or 13, and my mom said to me, "Oh you think you're a man then go ahead." I took the shot and man, I wanted to spit it out so bad but I wanted to be a man so I swallowed it as expressionless as possible. Looking back I can't believe some of the shit I did but it did happen and it cannot be changed. It was a lesson, and I'm grateful to be unbound, and faithful to God and helping others heal on our journey. The past is in the past, but I wouldn't change it for anything, because it's a part of what God had planned for me.

I remember working at the Huddle house, and I was so drunk I called out of work telling them I was dead and would return to work when I came back to life. It sounds funny, right? So by the grace of God, C. has managed to quit drinking liquor, and still drank beer. I know it's not sobriety but it's a step closer. His health is pretty bad. Here's a little to know about C. Our stories are similar; his large intestines is hanging down about seven inches outside of his stomach; he has tried many times to get help at the emergency room, and has been turned away; for screaming and hollering because they will not treat him, and he's in pain. What do you expect from such a man? I'm not saying alcohol is the answer, but someone needs to help this man recover physically so that alcohol won't be his go to, and he can legally be medicated.

C. has also mentioned he's experienced with drugs to numb his pain because he couldn't get help from any doctors. He was super close to his mother and took care of her. His brother for some reason thought it was a good idea to move her into a home, closer to where he lived, in a gated community. He took her cell phone from her. She was suffering from alhzimers so she couldn't remember anyone's phone number, and C. was left out in the cold. He couldn't reach her, and didn't know how or even where to find her. Chris's family knew that Chris's mother's health was deteriorating. Well, she finally passed away and left an inheritance that C. was cut out of, and for C. like me, it wasn't about the money, it was about the love he had for his mother. There was so much he wanted to tell her.

He went on to describe his mother as super momma. She made sure they were taken care of, and let's not forget she was a beautiful woman. She was once married to ""The Rock," so Chris's mother was hot, she had to be. Chris asked us for help. I had to work that day, but Weirdo rode the bus with C. to the emergency room. He didn't know where anything was in Austin Texas, and he detoxed for a few days. Weirdo left our phone number, and till this day we still stay in touch. We made a forever friend, and pray for him daily. We hope his brother opens his eyes one day, and gives C. what is rightfully his from his mother's inheritance. If you are C Williams brother and you just so happen to read this, your brother really loves you, and you guys need each other. Weirdo and I pray you find it in your heart to own up to your side, and both you and your brother can be at peace with each other before it's too late.

Chapter 44

ANOTHER DEVILISH EXPERIENCE

Another incident with the devil happened in Austin Texas—
which these incidents are just tests we have realized now from
God. Weirdo and I were at a bus stop and this guy saw us with
signs that read, "We broke down in Austin Texas, from Auburn
AL. and we need help getting a transmission, please help." This
stranger said apparently he didn't think we were trying hard
enough, and he asked how long we had been there, and we told
him. It was literally two weeks before asking us these questions.
He tried giving us a pack of trail mix nuts, and some other food.
We thanked him and didn't take it because we had left the same
church he had just left and got the same food he did. Then this
man literally flipped out. He was trying to put on a fake front

like I did during active addiction and act like his life was perfectly fine, and he didn't have any issues.

Weirdo and I were at this bus stop, and had our signs waiting to get on the bus. Then the guy goes on to yell, saying we should have already been at the staffing agencies which we had and should already have our truck fixed. This man was yelling at us to the point that he was shooting spit out of his mouth on us. All I could think to do was ask him if he was sober. Oh my God! It was like a war against Afghanistan. He was screaming at us to the point that I had to hold Weirdo back, and I kept telling Weirdo to calm down. You could clearly see the guy had been wearing the same thing for a few days but tried to make it look like he was doing better than everyone else and this was exactly how I was in active addiction later to learn I was no better than anyone.

During active addiction, I thought nothing that came out of my mouth was ever wrong, and felt I was better than everyone. I took a few steps back to reevaluate the current situation, and understood this man was struggling with substance abuse, and he was in denial—exactly the way I was back in July 2022. We prayed for this man. We prayed he gets on the right path, realizes his worth, and starts living right. This man was already in his late forties, and when I thought about it, it made me think he was probably in our situation in the beginning and lost his truck, or car you never knew. So in the end, we just prayed for his healing.

Remember that the devil is real, especially if you are in active addiction, and you're not strong enough to stand your ground, and keep your faith, drugs leave windows open to really evil things. Please believe before it's too late. We would have for you to live what we have already lived, and learned lessons from.

Chapter 45

A WOMAN AND HER DOG

So today is our Sunday, I will return to work tomorrow, when I'm off, Weirdo takes off from door dashing too. We like to go out and hangout with the homeless and actively using addicts in the streets, and we love spreading the word; sobriety is where it's at. There's just something about being around people like us, who have yet to realize they still have a chance. We love motivating them. We needed it at a time, and we were blessed to have each other.

We would love to give a shout out to Olivia; you know who you are. We want to let her know that just hanging out with us for the three hours she and her dog hung out with us is helping us grow, and teaching us more, so as we are making new friends, we are hoping all parties of all of our conversations are growing too. I want you guys to know that she has some really amazing stories, and she is writing a book herself. We can't wait to read it once she gets it published. I must remind you all it's hard as hell living on these streets. This woman was once married to a police officer, had what society would call a normal life, and when her husband (God Rest his soul) passed away, heartache got the best of her. She was never on drugs, didn't suffer from any mental illness. It is sad to note that there are a million and one different stories on these streets, and we are blessed to be the ones telling them for these people. We pray that Olivia and her dog are protected, and she finds her way out of these streets, with what I would consider a blessing to have experienced what she has and to rebuild her life in society, spreading peace, faith, and love.

There isn't a day that goes by that we don't learn something. Knowledge is everything. Let's come together and teach what we know to everyone around us, so that everyone learns, and society becomes more open to what isn't considered the norm in our society today. We told Olivia that if she wanted to because we know it's not easy being on camera and sharing her story, that on her own time she can record herself and we will post it. She doesn't have to show her face, but there's a lot of knowledge this woman has, and it can really and honestly help a lot of people out here. I really hope she comes through. We understand how sensitive and personal things are, and that is why my book is titled *Truth*. There are things I told in my book that have never left my mouth until I began writing. It feels really good to come clean and not have any fears. It's a huge burden off your shoulders.

When you approach anyone going through the struggle, make sure your intentions are pure, be as truthful and honest as you can because they deserve honesty. Remember why you're really out here. I want my light to shine on everyone. Don't fear anyone and keep your faith in whatever you believe in.

Chapter 46

PROCESS OF ELIMINATION

——

I've been working at Uhaul for two weeks now. Personally, I go into a job and I put my full commitment and dedication into it from day one. I love to learn, but I especially enjoy learning from people, and getting to know them. I can read people pretty well. I'm going to put my first impressions of everyone that I work with because I know that they will enjoy reading this part in my book. They are awesome people. Mr. Norbit, my manager, is one of the hardest working men I know. He and I have had conversations and he hasn't had a perfect life either. Just two years ago, he ended up getting really sick, and his medical bills by themselves came out to be 12 or 15 hundred dollars more than what his medical insurance would cover. Like me, he had child support.

Mr. Norbit was once married; at this time he was divorced. He ended up being homeless, and living out of his truck. He told me every morning he would wake up in his truck, put on a pair of duress pants, nice dress shirt and a tie, grab a newspaper, and hit up the local hotels that served breakfast and coffee in the mornings, and that's how he would eat his breakfast, and get his coffee. He would act like he was one of the tenants, to me this was brilliant, and I used to do this during active addiction in Alabama.

I remember right when my son started staying with me and my ex-marine. I wanted to show my son a little fun and at the time my son was probably ten years old, we would run in this hotel on Opelika road and treat ourselves to an awesome breakfast. My son laughed so hard and I miss him laughing. Mr. Norbit went through the struggle and now runs the U Haul that I absolutely love working at. His story made our situation not seem so bad. There's nothing like having a boss that has been where you are, and understands. He's an inspiration to me; he is a hard worker, and I look up to him.

Two of my most favorite people are Mrs. Bonnie and Mr. Clyde. They have been working for Uhaul for the past 25 years. They are amazing on the inside and outside. They are Hispanic, and they have a daughter that lives in Alabama. Mr. Clyde has shown me pictures of her and her husband—both of them are gorgeous. Mr. Clyde has always told me she got my back, and that in itself works wonders for me. Mrs. Bonnie tries to help me understand computer systems in the U Haul, and it's because she really wants me to learn, and she may not say but it's cool because she sees where I struggle almost instantly, and shows me the right way to do things. It means the world to me knowing or trusting the fact that there are still genuinely good people in this world. Nothing happens coincidentally. I know we didn't break down in Austin Texas by accident. God got us here for many different reasons.

Weirdo and I were in McDonald's one day and I was trying to get my free refill and the woman shooed me away and I felt hurt. Mrs. Bonnie and Mr. Clyde walk in and when I saw them I started crying but Mr. Clyde squashed that really quickly. Everyone at the McDonald's speaks Spanish, so did Mr. Clyde and Mrs. Bonnie. They squashed the coffee issue, and ever since we haven't had problems at McDonald's. It's weird because it seems like they always pop up when something is going wrong. They are always around, and if something goes on at work, Mr. Clyde already knew about it, though I didn't tell him anything, and he and I would talk about it. Mr. Clyde always tells me things like, "You guys are going to win the lottery one day, just wait and see." Little things like that give us the hope to continue living right, and spreading the good word. Mr. Clyde talks to Weirdo and it makes Robby feel included when this protector of mine feels left out and bless his golden heart. All I'm trying to say is these people really care. We love them.

The first week I worked at the U Haul, I had it rough. We had an assistant manager whom I won't give a name to but she wouldn't take accountability for anything and she loved to turn the heat on me whenever something would go wrong. I think she thought I was stupid. I'm the type of person that will take shit, sit back and watch, continue putting my full effort into my job, and continue to take shit, but after a while, I'll let my emotions get the best of me.

One day I asked this assistant manager if I could walk to the restaurant next door to grab a cup of ice. She agreed, and told me she placed an order at the same restaurant. Then she asked me to pick it up for her and told me to get her a cigarette as well. Remember this was the first week on the job, and I had no money. I did that for my assistant manager. The next day this assistant manager said to me that Mr. Norbit didn't want me going and getting ice anymore from next door; she said that he wanted me clocking out each time I go. I asked her if they clock out whenever other employees go and get food, and she shrugged. I later found out Mr. Norbit didn't say anything about it.

This woman was seriously going out of her way to give me a hard time. There would be times when she would ask me to go and shunt the trucks and we would get busy and other coworkers would come up to me and say they needed my help, and it wasn't like I wanted to try to help. So literally this woman kept drama at our store. I feel like I had enough going on and all I wanted to do was clock in at work my shift then clock out and figure out a way to resolve my truck issues, but this woman needed drama, and played me for stupid.

This assistant manager frustrated me. I honestly believe God put Weirdo and me in Austin Texas for many different reasons. I was hired at Uhaul to clean out what my boss didn't need. Mr. Norbit is a drama free man, and U Haul is a drama free establishment. This assistant manager, however, had me literally crying. I had it all in, and then I finally stood up for myself and told the assistant manager that if she wanted food she had to get it herself, and that I had coworkers that needed my help. I told her to quit blaming all her mistakes. She got furious in front of customers in the U Haul. She yelled at me, "I'm not one of these homeless people you can talk to however you want. You can clock out and get out of here. We don't need you." Right then I wanted to tell her, "A lot of these so-called homeless people you're talking about are more professional than you, and I would rather be homeless (which we are), than be categorized in a category with you or anyone that is at all like you."

At that moment I walked out and was crying. She continued to behave unprofessionally even after I had left. She felt she was showing off before her customers when in all actuality she was making herself look really bad. A part of me thinks I was an easy target and Mr. Norbit knew exactly what was going on at his store, but needed everything caught on camera so that the higher ups could see how this woman really was. I didn't clock out. I needed the money and I would be damned if I let this person win. Apparently, she had a lot going on, and by this time, I was growing and could understand that this woman had healing to do as well.

We all have a lot going on, and you still have no right to make someone's life miserable. Learn to deal with your personal problems at home. I have an issue when someone down right belittles you and makes you feel unappreciated and worthless; that is where my heart draws the line. I worked the rest of my shift and it was a difficult moment. I took a cigarette break, got on the phone, and told Mr. Norbit what happened and he told me, "Narcy, please hold it together and stay until seven in the evening. Usually I get off at six pm. He assured me everything was going to be resolved. The following Wednesday when I returned, the office was replaced with entirely different staff. My problem was gone; it seemed like everyone's problem was gone. The assistant manager was removed from our store, and honestly, it has been a breath of fresh air since.

Here's a little insight about my other coworkers. I am going to speak about the ones that have helped us through this journey fully. They are the ones I will cherish for the rest of my life. They will always have a place in my heart.

So we have C. and R.,I think they are two of the most decent human beings I know. They always have something positive to say; you could be having a bad day, but just seeing their smiles turned an awful day into an amazing day, and then there's Cici.

Oh my God! Where do I begin? She's a younger version of me. Then you have Carmel. I haven't got to know but he seems focused, and knows what he wants to do with his life. There is also Junior I would have to say he's my favorite. He's in school for business, and is thinking about entrepreneurship, which I think it's a brilliant idea. I wouldn't recommend going bowling with Jr. Just saying, he's a hoot.

When I get to work, I work from the minute I get there till the minute I leave. I don't bother anyone, and I appreciate the fact that I have a job. With sobriety, and life should come growth. In my case it does and I'm a 100% teamplayer and refuse to allow any drama in my life. I'm not sure about you guys, but I would say I have had enough drama in my life already.

Narrators insert:

My entire life I was the push over. People always walked all over me. I let them because when you're using drugs, you lose confidence in yourself and you just don't care. It feels so good to know that I have a voice, and I will stand up for myself. So with this journey, I'm learning to be strong and voice things when I know they aren't right. Remember what comes out of my mouth will only be the truth (La netta). Mr. Clyde told me not to let anyone talk to me in any kind of way. As I have mentioned before, he assured me he's got my back, and that speaks volume.

Chapter 47

OWN THE STREETS OR THE STREETS WILL OWN YOU

The first month Weirdo and I were here in Austin Texas, I was at the Cesar Chavez Library in Downtown Austin Texas. Weirdo went and got my printed documents I had typed up from the printer and he returned with this employee of the library. He was named S. and this man reminded me of how important this book/documentary I'm writing really is because living on these streets you tend to lose hope at times. S. came up to me with a beautiful smile, and told me that what I was doing was his passion. S. loves writing, I'm assuming, and we talked for a bit about my documentary and he went on to tell me if there was anything I needed at all, I should just let him know. For a minute there I felt like a superstar.

In the midst of our conversation, there was a man sitting at the table behind where we were standing listening and he cut in on our conversation and said he was out here making a documentary as well. S. returned to work, and the documentary man and I began comparing notes. He mentioned he and his wife were living out of a hotel because of COVID and they are working on getting a home. Documentary man was clean cut, and looked educated, professional and sober. We exchanged numbers and I got back to typing pages for my book. The only thing I don't like about the Cesar Chavez Library is that when I want to smoke a cigarette, I can't just go outside. I've got to descend down from the fourth floor to the first floor just to smoke. It is another reason why I'm going to quit smoking. I like working on my book on the fourth floor. I was typing for about an hour, and I asked Weirdo to take over. As I was putting my papers together to show him where to continue typing, I farted, and Weirdo went in to kiss me, and I told him to better watch out because I just let one rip, and there was this blonde headed young man that had heard what I said. He couldn't help but to laugh. Weirdo looked over at him and said that's why I loved this girl. The guy went on to say she had a sense of humor. I knew the guy was eavesdropping. He was getting frustrated in what it looked like he was trying to write his own music. I figured I could give the guy a laugh, why not.

The older I get, the more I realize I get my sense of humor from my father. If I'm a quarter of funny compared to what my father was then, I was hilarious. We called our new friend Beethoven. Weirdo would door dash most times when I would be at the library working on my book. Beethoven would watch my things every time I would go outside and smoke. I ended up telling Beethoven how Weirdo and I met, and this young man literally sat there and he listened, and it seemed like he enjoyed the story. We laughed. At this time, Weirdo was back from door dashing and the three of us began laughing. Beethoven and Weirdo hit it off because Weirdo likes music too, but what got me about Beethoven was he was human, a good one. I mean he didn't look at us any different because we were homeless and he treated us like people, like equals.

Come to find out Beethoven's grandmother has Alzheimer too, just like my mother. Well, my mother is dementia but that's just the early stages. Beethoven told us he would go visit her and play music for her, and she didn't necessarily know who Beethoven was or who he was exactly, but when she heard his music, she knew him as the guy that played music for her. You could see the love in Beethoven's eyes, when he talked about his grandma. It was what family should be like, or how I wished mine was. Well, I want to get back to talking about the documentary man. His documentary from what I collected was about how the city didn't put money in things he believed they should. He mentioned how Austin Texas had all these condemned buildings and how they continued to make Austin Texas bigger, but by doing so the states are neglecting the old Austin Texas.

From our conversation, I learned that Austin Texas puts on this big show just to make people think Austin Texas is getting bigger when it's actually not. I was trying to relate to the documentary man but honestly I couldn't. My main goal is to help make this world better by helping people. If I could start some kind of revolution, to bring mankind together for the better, I will.

Our world is crying; there's so much hurt and pain here. Anyways, two months into this journey, Robert and I met the documentary man again. We were sitting outside of Burnett

McDonald's and recording a live video for our documentary, and when we saw this man.

This man we saw was sweating profusely. He looked like he had on the same thing for two weeks, and had shaved in months. I shouted out to him. I was going to see if he wanted to have coffee with us and maybe compare notes. When I spoke to this man at the library, he was so passionate about his documentary, and so full of life. When I went to get his attention, he was walking fast and it was as if he couldn't hear me. He started to speed walk. Right then I got on my knees and started praying for him in the middle of McDonald's parking lot. It was like my knees just gave out, and I collapsed. Weirdo still didn't believe it was Mr. Documentary. I knew it was him; he just let the streets own him. He was what I called a zombie. I was there once, as a matter of fact; I was there for many years. I hurt for this man. When you lose yourself or anyone for that matter, you can look into their eyes and all you see is black. They are gone; the streets now own them. When you're out here, you can't let the streets swallow you, or else you will never get out of these streets.

About a month and a half later, Weirdo and I were inside of McDonald's on Burnet Road and in walks in Mr. Documentary. He went to sit at a table on the other side of McDonald's and then I guessed he realized who we were, and came and sat next to us. I asked Mr. Documentary how his documentary was going. He sure wasn't the Mr. Documentary we knew at the library a couple of months ago. Weirdo said it was like he was trying to fit into the streets. You could tell the streets did a number on him. He used the "N" wired and right then and there I looked at Mr. Documentary and said "I told you not to let the streets own you, and it looks like it did." I asked John if he was ok and he snapped back "I'm better than ever."

He wasn't ok. I asked him how his wife was and he said, "Oh well, she's gone just like everything else." Then I tried diverting the conversation from negative to funny, and I started making jokes about how I was going to be toothless, and Mr. Documentary pointed at Weirdo and said, "Well, you know what that means." (He was referring to a blow job with no teeth). Then he started laughing and I had to cut the conversation short before it got any more inappropriate. Mr. Documentary definitely changed in a total of two months. He was using, and went from being afloat to sinking. Mr. Documentary also said that he was waiting for the pawn shop to open so that he could go and pawn. I can't remember what kind of tool he had in the box sitting in front of him, but he was getting impatient because he was ready to go and pawn this power tool.

This incident brought back bad memories. I can remember being high with Weirdo. I'm pretty sure we were coming down and didn't have money so we were coming up with ways to get money and our dumbasses pawned his deceased brother's guitar. We would give anything to get that guitar. We would do anything to get that guitar back. At the time we were under the influence and we never in a million years thought we would be sober sitting in front of Torchy on West second street homeless in Austin Texas while writing a book about the consequences of our actions during active addiction. When we were using, we used to not have to deal with Pain, childhood trauma, drugs, and alcohol masked reality for a short time, just like a band aide covers a cut. We are grateful to feel every emotion, both good and bad now. So long story short our friend Mr. Documentary lost his fight with addiction. If I see him again, I've already told Weirdo we're going to grab a hold of him, and not let him go. In the blink of an eye, you can lose everything. Take Mr. Documentary, as an example. He lost his wife, job, hotel, and he just went on a downward spiral. Weirdo and I left Alabama before we let it get bad. We set out on a journey of a lifetime, and here we are.

Chapter 48

BULLIES

━━━━━━━━

During this journey, God has blessed me with the opportunity to have all my teeth removed, and get free dentures. M.A.P. Insurance is a God sent. Today I had another part of my process to getting dentures done so now I can only chew on one side. Once Weirdo and I left the Community center, it's another resource center. They hooked Weirdo and I with food. God knows we were hungry, and we ate, and we heated up five containers full of food at the seven eleven. The guy that managed the store was rude and wouldn't let me heat up much without bickering the entire time. This guy was rude.

Weirdo and I needed to go to the social security office because he finally got his birth certificate. Now we were on to the second step of getting his social security card, so that we could get his license and he could get a job, so we could get out of here sooner.

As most of you know I'm a very impatient person waiting to be called at the social security administrative office, which wasn't going to happen, so I told Weirdo that I was going to ride my bike to the Exxon, which was two miles away to get cigarettes and something for us to drink. Plus we were in a new area and I wanted to explore. I got to the Exxon and I couldn't believe what I saw. This was the first gas station that sold boiled peanuts. I was excited to get back to Weirdo and tell him, "We thought they only had boiled peanuts in Alabama, but the guy behind the register said it was an Alabama and South Georgia thing." After buying the cigarettes, I remembered that I left my lighter with Weirdo and by this time, I really wanted a cigarette. So I went back in and bought a lighter. I left my bike chain on Weirdo's bike, so I had to keep a close eye on my bike. I found a little nook to sit in to enjoy a whole cigarette before returning to Weirdo, and I wasn't aware of the middle school right across the street, and school had just let out. I was watching all the kids cross the street and come into the seven eleven. I think that was where all the cool kids met after school, to cuss and act like bad asses. It was a little window where all the kids waited on their parents to pick them up. These two maybe 13 and 14 year old boys saw my bike, but didn't see me sitting in this nook, as I watched them plotting to take my bike. I told them immediately that I was aware of their plot. They knew they were caught.

I told them that they better not even think about it. Then I watched the kids walk across the street and there was this heavy set black boy with crazy looking hair style. He walked toward the two kids that were plotting to take my bike, and yelled, "Hey, where's my money! You stole my money! You stole my money!" There was another overweight black kid among them. The other two started making comments like, "you're a fucking fat ass," and "why does your hair look like that?" Then they went on to call him, "Fat Albert," and that got me angry. I took as much as I could. I went to gather up my stuff and walked toward the road. Then I saw one of the two young kids hit the big kid from behind, and I threw my bike down, took off my sweater and started shouting, "Hey Hey, don't you dare put your hands on that boy again!" There were a couple of cheerleaders standing near them watching. I looked over at the girls and told them, "Girls only punks do that to people." I told the girls, "Karma is going to make sure the bullies get what they deserve when they get older." The girls agreed with me, and it humiliated the two bullies. I just wanted them embarrassed so that hopefully they would learn their lesson, and stop. I told the kid, "Forget that money they took from you, and in front of the two bullies, I gave the big kid $20.00. I know I didn't have it to give but I wanted the kid to not give up, and not get discouraged.

We have a big bullying problem in schools these days. My son was bullied and I wasn't there to protect him the way I know now that he needed me to, and I have to live with it every day. I know I was at this gas station at that exact time because God wanted me to open my eyes and learn from my mistakes. Parents, we need to teach our kids how to come together and be kind instead of what society has created. There shouldn't be clicks, cool kids, preppy kids, nerds, or band geeks, emo or emu. I'm not sure what they are called exactly. Kids are committing suicide at ages as young as eleven and twelve years old, so save your kids before it's too late. I pray that one day my son reads this and knows that I'm truly sorry. My kids mean everything to me, and I thank God every day for sobriety because now I get to feel these emotions that I forgot I even had.

I really hope this book is opening people's eyes. For the parents that aren't involved in their children's life, don't give up. You still have a chance, but you must get right with yourself before you can be right for anyone, especially your kids. Your kids need you. It may take a year for you to get back on track (or less, or more). It doesn't matter; time flies, use your time to get better because that year that you're not involved, beats not being in their lives, their entire lives. Trust me if you put in the work, God will put in triple.

Chapter 49

INTUITIVE

———

Weirdo and I have gotten used to being kicked out of everywhere we try to sleep, and I have made it a point to not post where we lay our head. It just seems like every time we post something that happens we get kicked out. It's getting cold out here and I still won't take this journey back for anything. We are fortunate to be going through this. We tend to want to share our story and share our door dash with everyone. I know this sounds crazy but sometimes bribing people with coffee warms them up to us and they open up and begin talking to us. Now everything makes me cry.

This woman was staring at me while she was standing in line and I felt something strange about her. I couldn't help stare back, and then tears kept streaming down my cheeks and I had to step outside to just cry. I had a feeling when she got her coffee she would come up to me and talk to me, and she did. We connected. I heard a voice, and it was the kindest voice, and it went like this, "excuse me, I'm an intuitive and I didn't mean to stare at you inside but I was drawn to you".

She said she had to tell me some things. She said she made a vow to Gaya (God) that no matter what anyone thought, if God worked through her, she made a vow to speak up. This intuitive was a beautiful African American woman, with beautiful long hair, and her eyes were a honey hazel. She was absolutely beautiful to me, and she smelled so good. She told me that there are going to be some decisions that will come my way that I don't need to be scared of. She also said that people are watching me, and lots of doors would open for me. If I was able to go into it without fear, she told me I was going to be ok. I think I was so quiet. I hadn't been that quiet ever in my entire life. I took what she told me straight to my heart. All that came out of my mouth was, "I am tired." It meant the world to me to hear this from a complete stranger, as she was talking to me. I couldn't take my eyes off of this gold earring that was in the middle of the road. Weirdly it gave me hope. I'm going for gold. Not silver, or copper. I've learned my worth, and I am going to make it out of this stronger and better than ever before. God is good all the time. If I never believed, I believe now, and this is the best feeling ever. I'm sitting here with the realization that everything I ever wanted is in me. It just took me 37 years to realize it.

I'm listening to Celine Dion, "That's just the way it is," and I'm still smiling, and nothing else around me matters. I'm in love with my life. In the beginning of my book, I mentioned "What's living, when you're not really living?" I am finally living life, yes, I'm homeless, but being able to feel all these roller coasters of emotions has opened my eyes to the world, and it's kind of like reading in between the lines but seeing, feeling, and understanding everything is a whole different level. If you're able to experience them you're blessed. I pray that all of you reading this make it to this level.

Chapter 50

RED SHIRTS ANGELS

Weirdo and I spend a lot of time downtown Austin Texas, getting to know all the homeless people, and so far we have met Ms. Dorothy, Isa, Simone, Marsha, Candlestick, Wes, Dottie, Frank, Deleon, and the list continues to grow. I'll tell you more about them throughout this journey. Everyone has a story, and I'm blessed to know their stories.

The cool thing about Austin Texas is they have people that walk around. They are employed by the city. They walk around cleaning the streets, spray paint off of public property, cleaning caca off of sidewalks. Some of these guys like Kevin for instance go around spreading hope. He inspires me, he knows a lot of the homeless by first name, and will stand around talking to us and everyone else. He really puts this genuine interest in getting to know everyone. He doesn't care if you're white or black He shares love, and verses from the Bible with everyone. Everywhere he goes there's this light that shines through him, and it's contagious. It can make anyone feel good. Weirdo and I call people like Kevin, "The Angels in Red" because they really are Angels. I think every state will or would benefit from such positive influence. This is exactly what this world needs, a reminder to be kind. No matter who you are, we're all just human. We are really becoming beautiful people, and I get excited just thinking about it.

Just a minute ago there was this homeless woman literally standing in the middle of the road. She was screaming, she had joggers rights and she was going to stand in the middle of the road if she felt like it. Then you hear another homeless person, yelling, "Get your crazy ass out of the middle of the fucking road!" Once again I felt this urgency to talk to this woman and bring her back to planet Earth. So I got up, grabbed my cup of coffee and started walking toward her. I shouted out, "Hey, do you want my coffee?" She declined my offer. Remember, I was in the middle of a busy four way street with this woman as cars were honking at us. I asked her for her name, and she answered, "I don't have a name." Then she said, "I don't want your coffee. I know you poisoned it. It's funny because during active addiction, I would always accuse Weirdo of poisoning my food and drinks, when really he didn't, and I was just paranoid.

This woman finally said, "My name is Abbott." I told her my name is Narcy, but she could call me Marcy, Darcy. It really doesn't matter. I answer to all of them. I was just trying to be funny. This woman started to walk close to me, grabbed my coffee and then told me her name was Michelle. This woman got out of the middle of the road and we both went our separate ways. Sometimes all it takes is asking someone their name instead of yelling at them and telling them: "Get your crazy ass out of the middle of the road".

Chapter 51

BUSY PEOPLE

▬▬▬▬

On my off days, while Weirdo would be door dashing, I love to get sugared up on coffee, and find a bench in downtown Austin Texas and watch people. If you just sit back and pay attention you can feel different energies coming off of different people. It's pretty exciting actually. It can also drain you and you can get extremely tired, upset, hurt, happy, all at once because people are going through so much and what makes it so sad is a lot of these people are living lives they don't even enjoy, and they aren't happy. They live this lives because that's the box society has incarcerated them in. That's all they know. So here's a theory I have come up with, and I truly believe it, and want you to think about it. They live each day doing the same exact thing their spirits/souls are screaming for freedom. So what do they do?

They live unfulfilled lives and their spirit travels to the next body until finally they evolve. Your spirit may live through many different life cycles, till it finally finds the freedom it desires. It's quite sad if you think about it.

So I find myself out here on these benches in downtown Austin Texas praying for these people. Never in a million years did I ever think this is what I would be doing. There's so much more to life than what everyone is imprisoned to think there is. These busy people need to take a break from these busy lives, and start living for once before it's too late. This guy just walked up to me as I was writing and asked for a cigarette. My pack was sitting in plain sight. Anyone that smokes would know I smoke menthol. He began saying, "Since you were willing to give me a cigarette even though it's menthol and I smoke non menthol, I won't take one of your cigarettes, but I will give you this dollar. If I had it, I'd give it to anyone. My life is not based on pride, possessions, or materialistic crap. You can always get things, but not always do you get acts of kindness, and that's truly what means the most to me.

Not even ten minutes later a homeless man was digging in the trash can right next to where I was sitting. He was looking for food, and I turned around and gave him the dollar I was just blessed with. There are a lot of homeless people out here that can't get jobs like Weirdo and me. Their appearance isn't acceptable in society. These people are looked down on. It's sad for those that are mentally ill, and don't know how to do anything about it. So when we are blessed with a couple of dollars here and there, we turn around and bless someone who could, "Really Really", use it. Yes, we need a transmission for our truck but we have learned we did it break down in Austin Texas for no reason. We are here to learn, and trust me when I say, we are learning, we are learning.

I was sitting on a bench in downtown Austin Texas. When I got up to pee, a construction worker came and sat on the bench right across from me. He was just staring at me while smoking a cigarette. I knew he was going to talk to me. He finally asked me what I was writing. I told him and he told me that we needed more people like me out here. I finally said to myself that I couldn't hold my pee anymore and I packed myself up and went into this beautiful restaurant and I parked my bike right next to the entrance. I knew it would be safe there; there were many restaurant customers sitting outside at the tables. I figured someone would be too scared to attempt stealing my bike. Just my luck, I had to go up three flights of stairs to get to the restroom, and it was like a maze trying to find my way back out of this restaurant. I ended up coming out of a completely different exit and started freaking out because my bike was unchained, and I can't find my way back to the front of this restaurant. I finally made it back around to the front, and Thank God my bike was still there.

Chapter 52

PROCESS

▬▬▬▬

I was sitting on what we call the worm—a huge snake looking thing right across from the seven eleven—doing my usual drinking coffee and working on my book. While using this hot spot, I checked out from the Cesar Chavez library that was overdue, as well as my laptop. Listening to "Tom McDonald's Sober," I haven't heard this song since the beginning of this journey. I literally broke down crying because Weirdo and I made it; addiction will be a battle that we will be fighting for the rest of our lives. We never surrendered. If you haven't heard this song, you must.

I have had three quarters of my teeth pulled. I have one more quarter and then my mouth has to heal for a whole month, and then I have two months to wait on a waiting list for dentures. God, I know you want me to learn how to be patient, but dang I know two months will fly by. It's already been about six months, and I don't know where that went. I need to just thank God that I'm fortunate to even be going through the notions. There are a lot of people who have to live with bad teeth. I'm going to be beautiful when all of this is said and done.

Weirdo was off doordashing and something strange happened. This guy stopped in front of me, and asked if he could take a picture of me. I gave him a peace sign, and he smiled and went on his way.

It's people like this man that give me the encouragement that I need to continue. God bless him. Weirdo, we believe made it in some kind of video. He said over here on Fifth Street they had some guys recording and while he was door dashing, he rode his bike right in front of them, and threw the peace sign. He was super excited, and I was for him.

Chapter 53

SENTIMENTAL STRANGER

After work one day, Weirdo was already downtown door dashing and I love my couple of hours alone. Before I catch the 803, or any of the three buses to make it to downtown Austin to meet Weirdo, I take this couple of hours to just meditate, and have conversations with God. I would sit outside of the seven eleven and literally admire the beautiful sky and feed the beautiful birds. It's amazing to be able to appreciate the little things God has blessed us with. God's good. Then a guy walked up to me and asked me about my bike and I was freaking out on the inside because I know bikes are like gold out here. I told him not to steal my bike, and he said stealing was something he didn't do. I promised to give him a cigarette if he didn't take my bike, and he promised he wouldn't take it. He then asked me if he could sit down with me, and I told him he could. He said he wanted to give me something and pulled out a picture. Well, it was a quote he had just made into art that read "Your inability to forgive will imprison you," and then he gave it to me. He quickly said he was happily married. And he and his wife were complete opposites but that they were soul mates—twin flames were his exact words. You know when people give me things I make it a point to cherish these things, and keep them close to my heart. It meant a lot to get this from a sentimental stranger. I hope if he's reading this one day he knows this.

Right when the Sentimental stranger said that, I realized we could have a conversation and I didn't have to worry about him hitting on me. So we started talking about astrology. And my attention was this metaphor he explained to me. He said we were both a daisy but we both have two different perspectives on ourselves and thought he was just a weed that dust gets trapped in its petals, and the sun never shines on me. I don't smell good, and then me being the daisy I could be grateful or happy. I could love how the sun shines right on me. When it rains, I get the perfect amount of rain that helps me stay beautiful. In all actuality, both of us are walking on the same side walk with two completely different perspectives but the daisy itself is neutral. The way a sentimental stranger thinks about everything is neutral. Which to me I never thought like that, but it makes sense to me because everyone has different ideas of heaven and hell. Heaven and hell is neutral to him but I have completely different views. It opened my eyes to a very interesting perspective. I love being out here and learning. Sentimental stranger told me he was kidnapped for four hours, and the people that had kidnapped him performed satanic rituals on him. He showed me a big and a small bite mark on his neck. He said that they literally sucked his blood, and he had PTSD from it. He told me that I would be the fourth person he actually told his story to. That he cried every time he shared his story; but with me he didn't have any fear to tell me about it.

He was also diagnosed with a disease that starts with a "B." It's a terminal disease. All I know is that when his body produced dead cells and he ate a salted pretzel his gums literally formed around the food he eats. So really his dead cells were taking over the good cells, which was unfortunate because he was so young. He also mentioned he's had over 100 seizures, which was mind boggling. He said his wife should be certified when it comes to seizures, because she was taking care of him. I'm just glad they have each other.

Sentimental stranger uses drugs, and he finds that a neutral choice as well. He's married to a woman with the same name as him, and right before we parted our separate ways, he told me his name, and I can't tell you guys his name. I hope I run into him again so Weirdo can meet him. I'm not going to lie. I was curious where he and his better half were living, and he told me they lived under a bridge. He started to walk away, and then turned around quickly and ran back to me, and said he never did this, but he wanted to sing a song for me that he made. He sang this beautiful song to me. He was in fact praising God and it was beautiful. He is definitely a sentimental stranger, but another friend from the streets that will hold a place in my heart. God bless him. In spite of all that he's going through, he still has faith, and that in itself is so powerful to me.

Chapter 54

B.O.B.

███████

This man right here holds a special part in our hearts, and he deserves a chapter. This man has been through hell and back. I'm surprised he's still going, but I've realized I'm not the only one with a sad story. Now you know that we don't have to follow the paradigm we were worn with. Bob, Weird, and I are living proof.

Just like myself, I was disowned when I shared my story, no one in my family believed it, but the truth hurts, and if the shoe fits, it's about fucking time the truth is surface. There's not a more peaceful feeling than the feeling of letting go of all the hell you have carried inside of you your entire life; it's a heavyweight thank God I don't have to tote it around anymore.

Here's something I heard in a Tom McDonald song, "The truth doesn't damage points of views that are legitimate." I believe in this 100 percent.

Bob is a victim of child molestation. He's currently 55 years old, and has been clean off of heroin for four and a half years now. This story must be shared. When Bob was a child, his stepfather who was Canadian would molest him in front of his mother, and she would stand there watching, and telling Bob not to fight it, and then Bob's stepdad would turn around and make Bob have sex with his own mother. Bob's mother and step dad were both alcoholics. He was the only kid out of his brothers and sisters who were molested. He was removed from his home and placed in foster care. Thank God for his uncle who was a police officer—who knew the signs of child molestation. Bob's uncle took Bob to the side one day, and asked him, "What's going on? You better not lie to me boy." He was a caring uncle.

Bob finally came clean and told his uncle everything that was happening to him, and his uncle took him to the emergency room, and had a rape kit test performed, and there was all the proof they needed. Bob was eight years old. This kid was disowned from his entire family, by no fault of his own. His mother ended up getting in a car accident and she lived the last couple of her years on earth as a vegetable, and for his stepdad, he was found in a car 36 hours later, after he was tortured—we do not know who—but Bob had said he knew where the weapon was and the clothes his father was wearing during his murder. Bob's stepfather deserved what he got. You do not deserve to live if you put your hands on a child.

God doesn't let that type of evil live comfortably on this earth and definitely, in the next life. It is extremely unfortunate what BOB has gone through. I truly believe he saves his best soldiers for his hardest trials and battles. If you guys got to meet

Bob, you would think he's one of the strongest people you will ever meet. This 55 year old man can out ride me on a bike race, and I am ashamed. I've got to get in shape. Weirdo and I promised him Weirdo's first bike we bought off the streets once Weirdo got a different one, which Weirdo scored. He ended up buying a mongoose from some guy on the streets for 22.00 dollars, and it's in better shape. Weirdo and I were so excited to get this bike to BOB. We knew we could find him if we went to the Cesar Chavez Library so Weirdo was determined to ride his bike and hold on to the handlebars on his other bike, and I would tote my stuff on my bike. We would get on a bus and go all the way across town, and make sure Bob got his bike.

Taz, our friend saw the bike before we got it to Bob, but we wanted to keep our word, that was something we were working on because during active addiction, there were so many broken promises, to so many people that meant the most to us, like my kids. I pray one day I can make it back to them, and they understand. It took me 37 years to understand what my mom went through and learn the truth about things I was lied to about my entire life. Well, Weirdo and I didn't break our promise to Bob. Taz is supposed to be leaving for treatment today, and we will go by the Gazebo and see if he left. I honestly believe God got a hold of him and will get him into treatment.

Bob was so excited to get the bike. Remember he's 55 years old, but he's still a kid at heart, and I think when he hangs out with us, we allow him to be that kid he missed out on when he was a child because of unfortunate circumstances. He was robbed of his childhood, just as I was. We are blessed to have met, and once again this is proof that nothing happens by accident. We all meet for a reason, and everything happens in perfect timing, trust me. God has a plan. Just have faith, it may take 55 years, or 37 years, like in my case, but God knows when the time is right. Bobs is a big teddy bear. If you didn't know him, you would almost always see him on a bench in front of Cesar Chavez Library, crocheting scarves for everyone, and blankets. He's very talented, and he's told me many people think he's gay, but that's not the case at all. He's lesbian, he will tell you. Whenever I'm around, he's so protective over me, and God, it feels so good to know that Weirdo and I are starting to make true friends; we're making our family. God is good. My eyes are literally tearing up as I type this. I understand my biological mother's situation a lot more now that I have lived and walked in her exact unfortunate footsteps.

I'm learning that there is such a thing as generational curses, and I am going to break the ones in my family, whether or not they stand by my side. I truly believe I am strong enough to fight all their battles. God didn't make me this tough for no reason. I'll be damned if either of my kids have to suffer anything like my mother or myself. As for my brother, I'll take his load. I just pray he opens his eyes and sees that I am his sister, and knows that I love him unconditionally. Nothing can stop me. I'm going to be the daughter my father knew I was and still believes I am. My father is proud, and that man will always be my hero. Meeting Bob and Taz, and the many others that hold a place in our hearts, are family now, and I promise you we will stick together like cement. We will be the family that all of us have always yearned for. God saves the hardest battles for his strongest soldiers. We are the chosen ones and we remain so.

Chapter 55

FINALLY AT PEACE

It has taken 37 years for me to find my peace and contentment. The peace that I have found is unexplainable. God brought me such peace. I catch myself sitting on sidewalks, or in buses with a smile on my face. I don't know exactly why it's there, but I know it's this overwhelming feeling of wonderful emotions. I am speaking for myself.

I may not have a home, or a truck that is running but I'm alive for once in my life. My tent is my castle. Instead of living, and not really living, I'm alive. I've done this sober thing two times before and never have I ever felt this wonderful about it. I finally found my purpose, and I'll let you guys in on what I am truly passionate about—what my soul desires. I am truly the luckiest girl in the universe. I have been fortunate to find myself, to be confident in who I truly am, and I'm able to not care what anyone thinks about me. I am a human being that deserves everything my heart has ever wanted. I am not that bad person a couple of people have managed to make me believe I was. Fuck them, and for all the dumb ass followers that went along to put out the little light that I thought I had , you're in for a rude awakening; it's about to be the fourth of July every day.

The fourth of July is Weirdo and my sober date. In my entire life my favorite numbers have been 3 and 7, and I'm not quite sure why. I am currently 37 years of age, and I'm finally free. Isn't this all somewhat strange to you guys? Growing up, I dreamed of Weirdo. God made sure he made everything in active addiction unbearable for the two of us together, but no matter what God made sure, he and I stayed together. We have overcome everything, and are looking forward to what the future has to offer. Weirdo is what I dreamed of in a man growing up as a child—his bone structure, attitude, charm, tan, torso, eyes, and hair, the way his feet look, even the way his armpits smell.

We both had 13 tattooed on us before we ever even met. We were divinely put in each other's lives at the perfect timing—God's timing. I finally got the protector I have desired since childhood. I fear no more, and with Weirdo, we can conquer all things easily. Both of us have been through hell and back, and he had this unconditional faith in me, that it took four years for me to appreciate, and learn to understand. I got his back, and he's got mine, and as I've said before, this was all of God's doing. We are soul mates. I pray that one day you will be as lucky as he and me to find your soul mates. Everyone deserves to be happy.

Narrators insert:

I put my entire being into this book, it is my first. I recommend you write it truly heals. I have grown so much, and it took me losing everything and everyone in my life to find my soul purpose. Nothing happens by accident. Everything that I went through was necessary for me to evolve into this beautiful human being that I have become. I have learned to love myself, and love everyone around me. It is possible to change your paradigm, and it is possible to heal. Never give up. You guys need to look out for my second book, because there will be hundreds of stories from people that I have been able to cross paths with, and their stories must be heard. You are not alone. I love you, when you think no one else may, and I don't even know who you are, but I love you. Believe, trust, and work hard for what you deserve, and you will get it. Don't let the devil win. Let's be a part of the solution, not the problem. Watch me make a difference in this world for the good. Humanity needs people such as you and me.

Made in the USA
Middletown, DE
31 March 2023

27406455R00121